Ian Pitt and Alistair Edwards

Design of Speech-based Devices

A Practical Guide

Springer

Ian Pitt
Computer Science Department
University College
Cork, Ireland

Alistair Edwards
Department of Computer Science
University of York, UK

British Library Cataloguing in Publication Data
Pitt, Ian
    Design of speech based devices : a practical guide. -
    (Practitioner series)
    1.Speech processing systems - Design
    I.Title II.Edwards, Alistair D. N.
    006.4'54
    ISBN 1852334363
Library of Congress Cataloging-in-Publication Data
Pitt, Ian, 1957-
    Design of speech based devices : a practical guide / Ian Pitt and Alistair Edwards.
        p. cm. -- (Practitioner series, ISSN 1439-9245)
    Includes bibliographical references and index.
    ISBN 1-85233-436-3 (alk. paper)
     1. Speech processing systems. I. Edwards, Alistair D. N. II. Title. III. Practitioner series
    (Springer-Verlag)
    TK7882.S65 P567 2003
    006.4'54--dc21   2002026864

Practitioner series ISSN 1439-9245
ISBN 1-85233-436-3 Springer-Verlag London Berlin Heidelberg
a member of BertelsmannSpringer Science+Business Media GmbH
http://www.springer.co.uk

Typesetting: by Gray Publishing, Tunbridge Wells, England
Printed and bound by Cromwell Press, Trowbridge, Wiltshire, England
34/3830-543210 Printed on acid-free paper SPIN 10792015

Acknowledgements

TrafficMaster PLC for the loan of a Freeway for evaluation.

Peter Jarvis of the University of York for assistance in evaluation of voicemail.

Series Editor's Foreword

Why did/do so many intelligent enemy automatons in popular science-fiction television series speak badly: "Y-o-u w-i-l-l o-b-e-y"? As this book illustrates, good synthetic speech is now widely used to adapt computers for blind people, as flight-deck aids for busy airplane pilots, for warnings at times of war, voicemail, synthetic telephone answering systems; and lately applications in cars (navigation systems, reversing and parking guidance and voice-controlled in-car computer systems). Our television automatons should move into the future, away from their medieval past (Why speak at all, with telepathy to consider? – except for the audiences' primeval listening ability).

Pitt and Edwards put the subject in context in their very practical approach to the topic, laying to rest the increasingly familiar knowns, and introducing the new useful contributions, along with health warnings. Already the challenge of creating the individual sounds that make up spoken words and sentences has been met. And so the new challenge is to investigate the length of phonemes, the pauses between them and the intonation curve they form. Or to put it slightly differently, effective speech communication systems require appropriate choices of words, clause structure, rhythm, pausing and intonation. If you want to understand the past, or find out where we are today, or think about the future of the world in this context, this book will address all of your needs (and therefore enable work on these systems to continue or start).

If you want to find out the speech-based knowledge required to build speech-based interfaces that take full account of these factors, this is the book for you. The book has numerous examples and case studies to underpin its Practitioner status. Even if you do not have the need to look at speech-based interfaces at the current time, this book is still worth acquiring in order to keep up with commercial changes and requirements and I recommend its clear, clean text to you. If you do need to look at this subject professionally, then you must have this book – at least until telepathy arrives!

Ray J Paul

Contents

Introduction

Until quite recently, synthetic speech was little more than a novelty to most people. It was used in children's toys and occasionally in executive toys too, and in gimmicky applications such as talking alarm clocks. Some computers could generate synthetic speech, but it was rarely used for anything more serious than impressing or amusing friends. The relatively poor quality of most synthetic speech made it unsuitable for more demanding applications.

For some people, however, the usefulness of synthetic speech more than compensated for any drawbacks it might have. Blind people were early and enthusiastic users of synthetic speech; it made computers accessible at reasonably low-cost, and that more than compensated for minor problems such as poor intelligibility and Dalek-like intonation. Pilots are another group of people who made early use of synthetic speech. Flying a plane may demand the whole of the pilot's visual attention, so it makes sense to convey additional information through another sensory channel, such as hearing.

It is only in the last few years, however, that synthetic speech has entered the mainstream, finding applications in a variety of areas from voice-mail systems to satellite navigation and traffic-avoidance systems. This move has occurred largely as a result of improvements in the technology, making synthetic speech more natural-sounding and hence more acceptable to a wide cross-section of potential users.

For a number of years, the principal challenge facing designers was to create phonemes – the individual sounds from which spoken words and sentences are constructed – that sounded as much like the phonemes in natural speech as possible. That challenge has largely been met, and phonemes can now be synthesized with very high levels of accuracy. However, effective speech communication relies on more than just the accuracy of the individual phonemes; numerous other factors are just as important, such as the lengths of the phonemes and the pauses between them, and the relative pitch of the phonemes and the intonation curve they form. In many ways, these are harder issues to deal with than phoneme quality because the number of variables is so great and there are few concrete rules one can follow. The settings of these parameters will vary from one message to the next, depending upon such factors as the sentence type (question, statement, etc.), the location of important information within it, and the tone of voice required (polite, cautionary, etc.).

In this book we will look at some of the issues facing designers of speech-based systems, and consider ways in which some of the problems may be overcome. We will begin by considering the history of the technology and its evolution.

1.1 Evolution of Speech Synthesis

Speech is often seen as an essentially human activity. Nevertheless, there has long been a desire to make machines that can produce speech-like sounds. It has only been in relatively recent times, however, that it has been possible to create reasonably human-sounding speech using machines. This has been due to the development of digital computer technology.

There are two principal approaches to speech synthesis. Text-to-speech (TTS) systems are a pure form of synthesis as the sounds are generated entirely by machine, and no human voice is involved. The alternative approach is variously referred to as copy synthesis or digitization and is based on recordings of human voices.

1.2 Text to Speech

At its simplest level, a TTS synthesizer can be depicted as in Figure 1.1. Text strings are fed into the system (in a computer-readable code, such as ASCII) and the synthesizer generates the corresponding sounds.

The basis of the synthesizer is a set of rules that translate spellings into sounds. These are the sorts of rules that children learn when they are first learning to read. They associate a sound with each letter of the alphabet and they learn that certain combinations of letters usually represent particular sounds ("th", "ch", "tion", and so on). In a phonetic

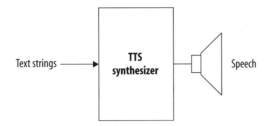

Figure 1.1 The basic design of a TTS synthesizer.

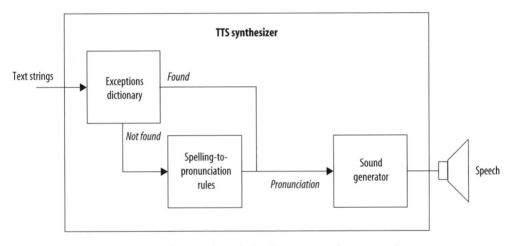

Figure 1.2 Stages of translation from a text string to speech.

language this might be quite straightforward, but English is not phonetic. Even the individual letters do not always have the same sound value (for example, is *c* hard, as in "cot", or soft, as in "cent" – or both, as in "circus"?). Some of these questions can be answered by additional context-sensitive rules, but in some instances English is just inconsistent. Just as a child has to learn that "It just is pronounced that way", so must the synthesizer be able to cope with exceptions. A good example is the spelling "-ough" which is pronounced differently in "cough", "bough", "bought", etc.

A TTS synthesizer therefore includes an exceptions dictionary. As each word is fed in, a search is conducted to see if there is a dictionary entry for it. If the word is found then the appropriate pronunciation is retrieved from the dictionary, but if it is not it is passed on to a rule base which applies the default spelling-to-pronunciation rules (Figure 1.2).

The quality of pronunciation will depend on the size of the exceptions dictionary and the quality of the spelling-to-pronunciation rules.

No matter how large the exceptions dictionary, TTS synthesizers will still make mistakes because some English words have the same spelling but different pronunciations. For example "wind" can refer either to an air current or a circular action, such as tightening the spring on a clock. In order to decide which pronunciation to use, the synthesizer would have to determine which meaning is intended – and that is beyond the capabilities of all current synthesizers.

Early speech synthesis systems required additional hardware because computers did not include a sound generator. Using hardware also relieved the main processor of the load involved in processing the data. More recently, it has become common for PCs to include a sound card. With a powerful processor, it is possible to do all the work of generating the phonetic representation of the speech that can then be converted to sounds by the sound card. Thus most modern synthesizers are implemented entirely in software.[1]

Quality of synthetic speech is usually measured in terms of how much like a human voice it sounds. TTS speech tends to sound somewhat mechanical. However the quality is improving all the time and some modern synthesizers produce output that is difficult to distinguish from human speech – at least over a phone line. The important feature of a TTS system is that it has an unlimited vocabulary; any word fed to it will be spoken. The synthesizer will even attempt the best possible pronunciation of nonsense words.

Beyond the accuracy of the pronunciation of the individual words, quality also depends on prosodic features, that is, qualities such as stress, rhythm, timing and intonation. Stress refers to the amplitude of the speech; it is one of the characteristics that are sometimes increased to accent a syllable.[2] Rhythm arises from the pattern of syllables in the

---

[1] When it was first released, the Apple Macintosh computer was ahead of its time in many ways and the very first model had a software speech synthesizer. The machine had sound generators built in as standard. It has been suggested that Steve Jobs, one of the founders of Apple, wanted the Macintosh on display at the model's launch to talk to him, and so he had a speech synthesizer, Macintalk, written.

[2] Stress is only one form of accentuation. There are others, some of which are often more important. The issues of stress, prominence, salience, etc., are discussed in Chapter 2.

utterance. Rhythm is related to timing, where timing can refer to the duration of syllables and also to the duration of silent pauses within the utterance. Intonation refers to the pitch patterns or "tune" of the speech.

A TTS synthesizer can apply rules to improve the prosody of its output. These are often improved by cues in punctuation in the input. For example, a comma is a cue for a short pause, while a full stop signals a longer pause. The full stop also marks the end of a sentence and this can inform the intonation. As we will argue later in this book, intonation is a very important feature of speech.

Allen et al. (1987) published a technical paper that presented the design of a TTS synthesizer in some detail, and proved very influential. It led to the development of the Dectalk synthesizer, which in turn has been the basis of many subsequent synthesizers.

1.3 Copy Synthesis

Copy synthesis amounts to recording words or phrases and playing them back under the control of the computer. While recording technology has been in existence for some time, this form of synthesis also relies on digital computer technology. The recordings are stored as digital data and can be retrieved and strung together.

The quality of copy synthesis speech depends on a number of factors. If the application calls for the speaking of one particular sentence, then that can be recorded with high fidelity, spoken by the most expensive actor, and the speech will be as near to perfect as possible. The problem is that a single sentence is somewhat limited in usefulness. At the other extreme, therefore, one might record a lot of individual words. These can then be strung together into a very large number of different utterances. Now the problem is that, although each word may have been recorded very well, when they are put together they will not sound natural. For example, the rules of intonation say that the way a word is spoken differs depending upon whether it occurs at the beginning of a sentence or at the end – or in the middle. If one plays a word that was recorded in the middle of a sentence at the end, it will probably sound wrong. It is also harder to apply other rules of prosody to digitized speech.

Some systems compromise between the two extremes using recordings of phrases. For example, on calling the Directory Enquiries service in the

UK, one hears a voice that says "The number you require is…", recorded as a single utterance, with good quality. This is followed by the telephone number, for example, "oh one nine oh four, four three two seven six seven". The digits of the number are clearly pasted together, but it is also noticeable that appropriate pauses are inserted (between the area code and the rest of the number) and that different recordings of the digits are used, so that the last "seven" is spoken on a descending pitch and differently from the previous occurrence.

Of course, the major limitation of a copy synthesizer is that it can only speak the words that have been stored. The more words stored, the greater the vocabulary – but the greater the memory overhead too. There will always be a limit, and this may be a significant limitation if, for example, the application calls for the speaking of proper names.

As with TTS synthesis, the inclusion of sound cards in most modern PCs means that copy synthesis can be implemented entirely in software.

For those who are interested in finding out more about the technical details of speech synthesis, further information can be found in Edwards (1991), Witten (1982) and Poulton (1983). The particular requirements of speech synthesizers for use by blind people are described in Blenkhorn (1995). There is an on-line speech synthesizer museum at http://www.cs.bham.ac.uk/~ipi/museum.html where samples of a range of current and historical synthesizers can be heard.[3]

1.4 Applications

It has taken quite a long time for synthetic speech to gain wide acceptance. This may be because the relatively poor quality of early synthetic speech systems limited its appeal. Many people found it fascinating to hear a machine talking, but if they were impressed it was (to paraphrase Dr. Johnson) not because it was done well, but because it was done at all. Had they been expected to listen to crude, mechanical speech on a regular basis or for long periods, they would no doubt have been considerably less impressed.

---

[3] Link checked on 29/1/02.

For these reasons, synthetic speech has until recently been used only in applications where it provided a very substantial advantage over other forms of output, or where no other form of output was available. Typical of such applications is the use of synthetic speech to adapt computers for blind people. For those who could not use a visual display, the only alternatives were synthetic speech or Braille (see Section 1.5). Braille terminals were expensive and could only be used by those who could read Braille, making synthetic speech the more popular choice despite its indifferent quality.

Another application in which synthetic speech has been used for some time is the communication of warnings and other information to pilots. Flying an aircraft is a demanding task, particularly in the case of fighter aircraft which sometimes have to be flown at low-level and high speeds, possibly while under attack from enemy aircraft. Such circumstances demand all the pilot's visual attention. If warnings or other information have to be communicated to the pilot at such times, it is potentially dangerous to use flashing lights or other visual alerts since these might prove distracting. It is much better to communicate the warning through sound. An additional advantage of sound is that people respond very quickly to sounds, whereas the response time to a visual signal is usually slower and depends upon the location of the change within the visual field. Buzzers and other non-speech sounds are suitable in some cases, but speech has the advantage that it can communicate far more information. For example, a simple tone might be used to indicate that the aircraft is running low on fuel, but using speech it is possible to indicate exactly how much fuel remains.

In modern aircraft, synthetic speech is used to convey a wide range of information. Numerous studies have been carried out in order to find out which of the various types of information that have to be communicated to a pilot can be conveyed adequately through speech, and which are best conveyed visually. In this way, the amount of information presented to the pilot visually can be kept to minimum.

As the quality of synthetic speech has improved and the cost has come down, many new applications have opened up. One of these is voicemail. Early voicemail systems did little more than function as answering machines, using pre-recorded messages. However, the ability to provide novel information – using speech of acceptably high quality – has led to an enormous increase in the features and flexibility of such systems. Modern voice-mail systems can report the date and time at which a message was left, summarize the contents of a voice mail-box, and much more. Many can also provide additional information, such as allowing staff to check share prices and other corporate information.

Another application in which synthetic speech is increasingly being used is in the provision of commercial and other information over the telephone. Until recently, most such services used recorded speech. This is fine in applications where the recorded information rarely changes, but time-consuming and inefficient in applications where the information changes regularly and the recordings have to be updated each time. As the quality of synthetic speech systems has improved, many companies have found it more convenient to store the information as electronic text and use a TTS system to turn it into speech. Using this approach, the information can be updated simply by editing the text.

The use of speech in cars still lags some way behind its application in air-craft, but the situation is changing rapidly. While driving a car may be less demanding than flying an aircraft, it nonetheless requires that the driver devote a lot of visual attention to the road ahead. Thus the arguments that apply in aircraft cockpits apply here too – if any additional information that is required can be supplied using sound rather than visual indicators, there is less risk of distracting the driver from the all-important visual task.

One reason why synthetic speech was not widely used in cars until recently may be that the benefits are not as obvious as in aircraft. The advantages of using speech in aircraft cockpits are so great that pilots were prepared to put up with the relatively poor quality of early synthetic speech systems, but for motorists the advantages are less obvious and many may be unwilling to use it unless it actually sounds enticing. The situation may not have been helped by the inappropriate use of speech in some early systems (see Chapter 8), perhaps leading motorists to conclude that speech was just a gimmick and had nothing of value to offer the motorist.

In the last few years, however, speech has been used in an ever-increasing range of applications in cars. Many cars now come equipped with satellite navigation systems that use speech output, and many motoring accessories use speech too (such as the traffic-avoidance system discussed in Chapter 7). A number of manufacturers have integrated speech synthesis into the control systems of a vehicle, enabling the driver to obtain spoken information on parameters such as speed, fuel-level, oil-pressure, etc. A few have gone further and included systems that allow the driver to control features such as the audio and navigation systems using voice commands.

The applications mentioned here are just a few examples, and the range of applications in which speech is being employed is increasing all the time. Some possible future applications are discussed in Chapter 8.

1.5 Applications for Blind People

The ever-increasing use of computers in almost every aspect of our daily lives has presented both problems and opportunities for blind people. Prior to the introduction of computers, many jobs were closed to blind people because there was no simple or obvious means by which the necessary tools and information could be made accessible. Many tasks involving book-keeping, for example, could be performed by a blind person if the records were kept in Braille form, but few employers were prepared to do this, especially if they were also employing sighted people on related tasks and would therefore need to keep parallel sets of records in Braille and print form. For these and similar reasons, blind people were all too often forced into a narrow range of relatively menial jobs – that is, when they could find work at all.

The introduction of computers changed the situation considerably. The first generation of business and commercial computers had command-line user-interfaces, in which all the interactions necessary to use the operating system were based upon text. These computers were relatively simple to adapt for blind people.

It's not essential to be able to see in order to type (even sighted typists are taught to work from touch alone), so text could be input using a standard keyboard.

The output from a command-line system also consists entirely of text, and this could be made accessible to a blind user through speech synthesis or Braille. A Braille display typically consists of an array of tiny pins embedded in a panel, arranged so that they can be raised or lowered rapidly using (e.g.) tiny electro-magnets. Braille displays have a number of advantages over speech, including the fact that the pins can be left in a particular configuration for as long as is required, allowing users to read and re-read material until it has been absorbed. However, they are also much more expensive than speech-synthesis systems, and generally less reliable. An additional problem is that they can only be used by people who can read Braille, and in practice only a tiny percentage of blind people are proficient Braille readers.[4]

For all these reasons, speech synthesis is more widely used than Braille displays. For a long time, blind computer users had to purchase separate, hardware speech-synthesizers, but the introduction of sound-cards with built-in speech-synthesizers has removed the need to buy separate hardware. This lowers the cost still further, since all a blind user needs to purchase is some software to drive the speech synthesizer in the sound card.

The software used to convert visual displays into speech (or Braille) is known as a screen-reader. It is loaded into memory when the computer is started-up and runs in the background while the user is running other programs.[5] A screen-reader for a text-based system allows the user to move around the screen (using the cursor keys, for example) and select sections of text to be displayed. Most can also be set-up to provide a number of other functions, such as warning the user when the screen display changes, or monitoring a particular area of the screen until (for example) a dialogue-box appears, and then reading-out the text in the box.

The introduction of Graphical User Interfaces (such as MS Windows) has made it far more difficult for blind people to use computers. While some operations (such as inputting text) continue to be performed using the

---

[4] Gill (1993) found that only around 2% of blind people in the UK read Braille. There are a number of reasons why the figure is so low. One is that Braille is difficult to learn, and is most likely to be mastered by those who start young. People who lose their sight later in life are far less likely to learn Braille than those who are born blind, or who lose their sight at an early age. Another contributing factor is that many people lose their sight as a result of conditions (such as diabetes) that may also damage their sense of touch.

[5] A few attempts have been made to produce hardware screen-readers. These use an external processor rather than running the screen-reader software directly on the user's computer. The necessary information is obtained from the user's machine by means of a connection to one of the standard ports, usually the monitor port. Where necessary, OCR techniques are used to recover textual information from screen bitmaps and other forms of graphical output. Hardware screen-readers offer a number of potential advantages over software screen-readers, among them the ability to continue providing feedback when the user's system malfunctions. However, they also have a number of disadvantages, not least their significantly higher cost and the difficulty of gaining external access to all the necessary system information. For these reasons, virtually all screen-readers in current use are software-based.

keyboard, many important operations now require the use of a mouse. These include such fundamental operations as selecting and launching applications, copying and deleting files, creating folders, and selecting areas of text for cut-and-paste operations. However, using a mouse successfully requires continuous feedback about the position of the cursor on the screen, and there is no easy way of providing this information to blind people.

Despite the obvious problems, a number of manufacturers have developed screen-readers that work with Graphical User Interfaces (GUIs), converting windows, icons, etc., into speech or Braille. Most do not rely on the mouse at all but allow the user to move the cursor around the screen using the numeric keypad. To facilitate this movement, the screen display is not regarded as a continuous space but is divided up into a series of horizontal lines, with the cursor jumping from one to another in response to presses of the vertical cursor keys. Individual lines are subdivided according to window borders, so that asking the screen-reader to read the current line will cause it to read to the edge of the window but not into an adjacent window on the same line. Various "hot-keys" allow the user to jump to other areas of the display, such as the menu bar, the desktop, or to other windows.

The approach generally taken is to have the speech synthesizer read out whatever is under the cursor. This is fine for text but obviously poses problems with icons and other graphics. One solution is to sort graphical items into one of a number of categories and then identify the category using speech, for example "application", "file", "folder", etc. This can then be followed by any text title attached to the icon so as to produce a composite description such as "application – word processor". However, graphics that are not recognized by the operating system (for example, a graphic created with a drawing package) pose significant problems. Some attempts at adapting GUIs have dealt with this problem by using a single generic description (for example "graphic") to describe all unrecognized graphic items. More sophisticated approaches involve image recognition, but these are still in their infancy.

As the preceding passage suggests, considerable problems remain to be overcome in order to make GUIs fully accessible to blind people. Possible solutions to some of these problems are considered in Chapter 8.

A number of companies and other organizations have developed speech-based software specifically for blind people, for example, talking calculators and word-processors. Since they are designed from the outset to use speech, such applications are usually much easier for blind people to use than applications that have been designed for use by sighted people. However, a major disadvantage of specialist software is that the market is relatively small, and in consequence such software is usually less well supported and less frequently updated than mainstream software. Thus users of such software may find themselves using applications that are out-of-date and incompatible with those used by the majority of people. For this reason, most organizations developing software for blind people have concentrated on trying to create generic adaptations for existing software.

However, there are a number of areas in which specialist speech-based applications can be of great help to blind people. Some of the devices that are sold as novelties to the general public can be genuinely useful to blind people. Examples include talking clocks, kitchen-timers, remote controllers, and so on.

1.6 Limitations of Current Design Methods

Current speech-synthesis systems offer very good speech quality, but effective speech communication requires more than this – it requires appropriate choice of words, clause structure, clause length, rhythm, pausing and intonation. At present, these choices are often made in a fairly ad hoc fashion. Decisions concerning wording, clause structure and clause length must take into account both general interaction requirements and the constraints governing spoken communication. However, such factors are rarely given the attention they deserve. Interaction facilities are often determined more by the underlying technology than by the requirements of the user, while choice of wording, etc., is often based on assumptions derived from written language that may not be appropriate to spoken language. Models have been developed that can be used to predict certain elements of prosody, but they are incomplete and are not easy to apply in practice.

This book sets out to provide engineers and others with the knowledge needed to design speech-based interfaces that take full account of these factors.

Background and
Previous Research

2

It is the quality of synthetic speech – that is to say how similar it is to human speech – which makes the first impression (good or bad) on listeners. Speech can be analyzed at the *segmental* level (where the segments are words or syllables) and the *supra-segmental* level, which is concerned with structures, such as sentences. Quality at the segmental level largely amounts to how well words are pronounced. This book is not about the technology of speech synthesis (there are plenty of other books which are, including Keller, 1994; Dutoit, 1997; Edwards, 1991) and so is not primarily concerned with how segmental quality can be achieved. Nevertheless the quality of speech affects how it can be used and some experimental results are reviewed in this chapter.

In many ways, supra-segmental quality is harder to achieve, and it is some of the theoretical results in this field that are reviewed in this chapter.

Written language – and the verbal component of speech – have been extensively studied within the disciplines of linguistics and natural language processing. It is complex and, though still not fully understood, a good level of comprehension has been achieved through such techniques as syntax analysis. Yet written language is very different from spoken language. This is easily illustrated if one ever reads a written transcript of a spoken conversation. In speech we do not always pay much attention to matters such as sentence structure, and yet we understand each other well. Conversely, if we hear someone reading out a written paper, we immediately recognize that this is something that has been written down, and is not a speech nor part of a natural dialogue.

Linguists have developed formalisms to describe the structures of written language. They also use notations to annotate transcriptions of spoken language to mark pitch, timing and stress. However, such notations are very specialized and of use only to linguists. They are used mainly as an analytical tool, as a way of examining people's speech, rather than as a way of prescribing how an utterance should be spoken. (An exception is the use of stress marks in a dictionary to aid people to learn how to say a word.) Text that is not annotated in this way (that is to say, the vast majority of existing text) retains a level of ambiguity. For instance, the sentence:

> Robert does research on drugs

can be read in two ways, either implying that Robert is a pharmaceutical researcher or that he is involved in nefarious activities. In speech the intended meaning should be apparent, depending on whether the stress is placed on the word "research" or "drugs".

While perhaps frustrating to the designer of speech technology, the flexibility and ambiguity of language can be a source of interest in other contexts. A playwright can hint to the actor how a line should be spoken ("excitedly", "sullenly" or whatever), but the final interpretation is left to the individual – and would it not be boring if Shakespeare had been able to prescribe exactly the location and length of every pause in (say) Hamlet's "To be or not to be" soliloquy?

It is also important to remember that most human dialogue takes place in a face-to-face context, where the spoken component of the dialogue is accompanied by important, information-bearing gestures of the face and other parts of the body. However, speaking machines do not have that communication channel, so dialogues become more like telephone conversations in which the verbal channel alone is available – and consequently there is greater scope for errors and misunderstandings. It is thus all the more vital to get the non-verbal component of the speech "right", and so avoid communication errors and breakdowns.

What makes a good orator? The subject of a speech is an important part of its appeal, yet there are those speakers who seem able to make an engaging speech on almost any topic. Choosing the right words is clearly vital, pitching the talk at a level that is meaningful and interesting for the audience. But beyond what the speaker says is the way in which it is said. There is a richness of meaning and nuance that is communicated in a non-verbal form in any speech. This meaning is encapsulated in such properties of the speech as its timing and intonation, characteristics that can even be altered in such a way as to vary the meaning of two statements consisting of the same words.

A natural speaker knows how to use these variations instinctively. Students (at drama school, perhaps) can be taught them at an emotional level, but to try to encompass these properties in synthetic speech we need a more formal understanding of the variations and their effects.

In this chapter we review the important non-verbal components of speech and some of the attempts that have been made to characterize those aspects. This will lead on in subsequent chapters to an examination of how we can attempt to capture the important features in synthetic speech.

2.1 Pausing and Rhythm

Sometimes in our speech we consciously insert pauses: for breath, for ironic or humorous effect, or perhaps to allow listeners time to think about what we have just said. But these are only the most obvious of the numerous pauses that litter human speech. Whether we are aware of it or not, we insert pauses between almost everything we say – between sentences, between phrases, between words. Some of these pauses serve obvious purposes, but most appear to serve principally as cues to help the listener disentangle the meaning from a string of words.

Just how pauses aid speech comprehension is still not fully understood, and a great deal of research is being carried out in this area. Nonetheless, most linguists now accept that pauses play a crucial role in speech comprehension. This belief is backed up by studies which show that inserting inappropriate pauses, or even just swapping around the positions of pauses within a speech string, significantly impedes speech comprehension.

Pauses can be broadly categorized into two groups: grammatical pauses, which separate one clause from another, and non-grammatical pauses, which occur between the elements of a clause. We normally expect the pauses that occur within clauses to be shorter than those that separate clauses, and where this is not true the speech becomes more difficult to interpret. Reich (1980) found that moving a short pause to an inappropriate place in a spoken sentence added several seconds to the average time taken by people to understand and respond.

However, it is not simply the case that grammatical pauses are always of one length and non-grammatical pauses of another. While grammatical pauses are, on average, longer than non-grammatical pauses, both types vary in length over a quite a wide range. This variation can be explained largely in terms of rhythm. Natural speech has a rhythm that is almost as well defined as that of music, and pauses (along with words) vary in duration to allow words to fall on the appropriate beats of the rhythm.

The role of prosody in spoken language, and in particular of intonation and rhythm, was explored by, among others, M.A.K. Halliday. In a series of articles published between 1963 and 1970, he examined the relationship between prosody and information structure in spoken British English (Halliday, 1963, 1967a, 1967b, 1970). Drawing upon extensive analyzes of recorded speech, Halliday argued that prosody performs a number of functions, one of which is the delineation of tone groups. A tone group in spoken language is roughly analogous to a clause in written language.

The rhythmic structure of spoken English, as defined by Halliday, is illustrated in Figure 2.1.

At the top level is the sentence, or perhaps more correctly, the *breath group.* A breath group is a passage of speech that is preceded and followed by an intake of breath. Breath groups are in most respects identical in function to sentences in written speech, and the final breath can be thought of as the spoken equivalent of a full stop. However, there are occasions on which breath groups differ from sentences, usually because the speaker constructs a sentence that is too long to be spoken with a

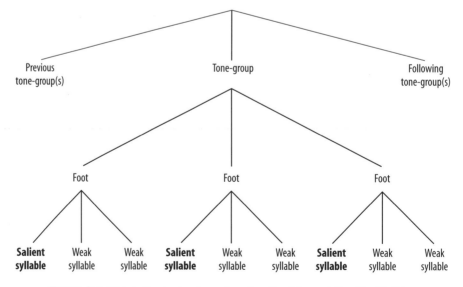

Figure 2.1 The rhythmic structure of spoken English, as defined by Halliday.

single breath. On such occasions the speaker may have to break the sentence into two or more breath groups, using rhythmic and other cues to tell the listener that the intermediate breath does not signal the end of the sentence.

Within the sentence (or breath group) are a number of tone groups, each of which, as noted earlier, is roughly equivalent to a clause. Each tone group consists of one or more subunits called *feet*. These may be compared to the bars into which a musical phrase is divided. As with musical bars, every foot has roughly the same duration as every other foot. Thus the foot can be regarded as a rhythmic unit. Some tone groups contain only one foot, but most contain three, four or more, and in rapid, informal speech the number may rise to as many as ten or twelve.

Each foot consists of one or more syllables which may be compared to the beats in a musical bar. Just as in music, where the first beat of the bar carries more weight than those that follow, the first syllable in a foot is of more importance than subsequent syllables. It is sometimes known as the stressed syllable, but to avoid confusion with other forms of stress found in spoken language the term salient syllable is preferred. The *salient syllable* may be followed by one or more weak syllables which carry no stress.

Salient and weak syllables carry different types of information, reflecting a linguistic distinction between *content* and *function*. Content words are essential to the understanding of a piece of text or speech, and include things like nouns, verbs and most adjectives. Function words are those that can be guessed from the context; if you remove all the function words from a message it should still be possible to recover the original message. Words that fall into this category include "a", "the", "of" and many others. Function words are the ones that speakers naturally drop when economy of words is important, such as when one is paying for them in a telegram, or when an utterance is urgent, such as a warning. For instance, the message "I will arrive on the 2:30 train, but my luggage will arrive on an earlier train", might become, "arrive 2:30 train. Luggage arrive earlier train". The function words have been omitted, and the length reduced by 56%. A list of words usually regarded as function words is shown in Table 2.1.

Single-syllable words of the content class are almost invariably placed on salient syllables, while single-syllable words of the function class are placed on weak syllables. In the case of polysyllabic words, accented syllables become salient while non-accented syllables become weak.

Table 2.1 List of function words

a	he	them
almost	her	themselves
an	him	then
and	himself	they
are	his	those
as	however	though
at	I	thus
because	if	to
been	in	until
but	is	very
by	me	was
can	might	were
could	more	while
do	my	will
doing	of	with
done	on	withdraw
for	or	withdrawal
from	she	within
had	since	without
has	the	would
have	their	you

Thus "April", which has its accent placed on the first syllable, will normally be spoken with the "A" on a salient syllable and the "pril" on a weak syllable. "July", which has its accent placed on the second syllable, will normally bespoken with the "Ju" on a weak syllable and the "ly" on a salient syllable.

By way of example, consider the following sentence:

Janet lifted the box

The nouns "Janet" and "box" and the verb "lifted" are all content words. "The" is a function word. Therefore "Janet", "lifted" and "box" will all be placed on salient syllables while "the" will appear on a weak syllable. "Janet" and "lifted" each have two syllables, but in each case the stress is on the first syllable. Thus this sentence would normally be spoken with the following rhythm:

Janet | lifted the | box

Each foot contains a different number of syllables (two in the first foot, three in the second, and one in the third) but despite this all occupy roughly the same amount of time. This is because the foot containing the word "Janet" is padded (either by lengthening the second syllable of "Janet" or by inserting a brief pause) so that it occupies the same amount of time as the following three-syllable foot. The result is that the three salient syllables – "Ja", "lift" and "box" – are spoken at regular intervals, thus creating a rhythm.

2.2 Intonation

Research suggests that the natural rise and fall in pitch over the course of a sentence serves, along with pauses, to help delineate clauses and so aid comprehension. It also helps the listener to determine where they are within the sentence, thus allowing efficient use of resources such as memory.

Analysis of human speech has revealed distinct prosodic patterns, among them a tendency for the pitch of the voice to rise fairly rapidly at the start of a clause, decline slowly throughout the clause and then fall sharply at the end of the clause. This pattern was identified by, among others, 't Hart and Cohen (1973) who christened it the "hat" pattern on account of its shape.

Where several clauses follow one another to form a sentence, the pattern is repeated for each clause but with a steady reduction in the average pitch of successive clauses. This is illustrated in Figure 2.2. It can be seen that the pitch rises to its highest point at the start of the speech and reduces steadily thereafter, with each successive clause having a lower average pitch than the previous clause. The pitch then drops sharply at the end of the final clause (unless the final clause is a question, or one of the other types of sentence that have a rising intonation curve).

This characteristic variation in pitch is found in many languages but not all. The principal exceptions are Tone Languages, in which the meanings

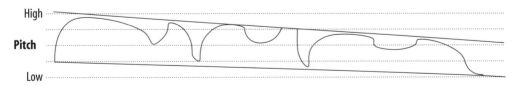

Figure 2.2 Characteristic variation of voice pitch over a linked succession of clauses (example taken from Vaissiere, 1983).

of some words vary according to the pitch at which they are spoken, and a few languages in which pitch is used to indicate a change of tense or other change of grammatical function. Around half of the languages in the world are tone languages, among them Zulu, Thai and Chinese (both Mandarin and Cantonese). Languages in which pitch is used to indicate grammatical changes are much rarer, the principal examples being Twi, Bini and a few other West African languages (Crystal, 1987). Among languages in which pitch is not used to indicate meaning or grammatical function, however, the type of intonation pattern described above is widely found. This group includes most modern European languages (Vaissiere, 1983).

Where a sequence of clauses is found, it usually displays several distinct characteristics:

● There is a steady fall in the average pitch, i.e. each successive peak is lower in pitch than the previous peak and each successive trough is lower in pitch than the previous trough.

● There is a steady reduction in the pitch range used, with the first rise and fall covering quite a large pitch range while successive rises and falls cover a progressively lower pitch range.

● Before the first rise, the pitch remains relatively steady for a short period. This is known as *postpausal lengthening* (because it follows the pause that separates this clause from the previous one).

● After the final fall, the pitch remains relatively steady for a short period. This is known as *prepausal lengthening*.

A number of studies (for example, Nakatani and Schaffer, 1978; Streeter, 1978) have shown that this rise and fall in pitch helps the listener segment the speech stream into phrases, and that missing or inappropriate pitch cues increase the time required to assimilate the speech and/or increase the likelihood of errors.

Many linguists believe that intonation curves serve not only to indicate the boundaries between tone groups but also to indicate the position of the most important information within each tone group. According to this analysis, each tone group contains one item of information that the speaker regards as important and, optionally, a number of items of supporting information. Intonation is used to tell the listener which is the most important information and which is the supporting information.

Halliday, for example, notes that tone groups in natural speech generally exhibit one of a fairly small number of intonation patterns. These patterns all follow the basic "hat" pattern, but the central part of the curve may start or end at either a high or low pitch and have different pitch curves depending upon the type of utterance (statement, question, directive, etc.). However, all have two characteristics in common: they can be divided into two distinct sections (for example, a section of rising pitch and a section of falling pitch), and the boundary between the two sections, the point at which the pitch changes most sharply, occurs at the point where the most important information is placed. Halliday uses the term *pitch-prominence* to describe the marking of important information in this way.

The nature of a tone group, as defined by Halliday, and its relationship to other features of spoken language structure, is illustrated in Figure 2.3.

A tone group comprises either one or two subsections known as segments, each of which comprises one or more feet. The tonic segment (sometimes referred to simply as "the tonic") is present in all tone groups. It contains a piece of information that the speaker regards as being more important than anything else in the tone group. This item of information will be placed right at the beginning of the tonic segment. In some

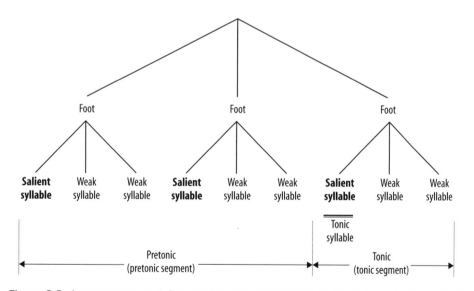

Figure 2.3 A tone group, as defined by Halliday, showing the division into pretonic and tonic segments.

cases the important information may be the only information in the segment; in other cases it may be followed by less important, supporting information.

In some cases the speaker will judge it necessary to include supporting information before presenting the important information. In these cases the tonic segment will be preceded by a pretonic segment (sometimes referred to simply as "the pretonic"). It is common for the tonic to be placed towards the end of a tone group, in which case it will be preceded by a pretonic that may be considerably longer than the tonic. In other cases the tonic is placed right at the start of the tone group and there is no pretonic.

2.3 New versus Given Information

We have noted that each tone group contains one item of important information, but we have not yet discussed what makes an item of information "important"; it is important because it is "new" to the listener. The speaker identifies material that he or she regards as new and builds each tone group around one such item.

For example, consider the sentence used earlier:

Janet lifted the box

If this statement were made in response to the question

Who lifted the box?

then "Janet" is new information. When spoken, we would expect "Janet" to be given pitch-prominence.

Halliday defines new information as follows. It is new, he suggests,

> … not in the sense that it cannot have been previously mentioned, although it is often the case that it has not, but in the sense that the speaker presents it as not being recoverable from the preceding discourse. (Halliday, 1967a, p. 204)

Thus, the new information around which a tone group is built may contain entirely new information – information that the listener has not encountered before – or information that has been presented previously but has not been mentioned for some time and which the speaker feels it necessary to re-introduce into the discourse. A valid test of what is and is not new information can be obtained by applying the criterion, "Present in the listener's consciousness" (Chafe, 1970). If a speaker judges that a piece of information he or she wishes to convey is not currently in the listener's consciousness, it should be presented as new information.

The opposite of new information is "given" information. In the example above, all the words other than "Janet" are given information. Halliday (op. cit.) defines given information as that which is treated by the speaker as being "recoverable either anaphorically or situationally". In other words, it is information that the listener should be able to remember if prompted (e.g. through the use of a pronoun such as "he" or "she" to represent a previously mentioned full name) or deduce from the context. Thus given information is that which has already been mentioned in the discourse or which forms an integral part of the topic being discussed.

The distinction between old and new information is critical to any understanding of the nature of spoken English because it underlies such observed phenomena as intonation, stress, word order and the use of anaphoric devices (Dahl, 1976).

2.4 Length of Utterance

We have noted that speech usually consists of a series of tone groups, each of which contains one item of information, and we have seen that the number of tone groups we can string together into a single sentence is usually limited by the need to draw breath. However, there are some other limitations on the length of speech strings that we should be aware of, principally determined by our memory capacity and the presence or absence of distracting sounds.

2.4.1 Primacy and Recency

The literature on language and memory suggests that if we hear a long speech string and then immediately try to recall it, we are most likely to remember the first few items and the last few items. The items in between will be recalled less reliably. This effect has been noted by a large number of researchers using various stimuli, including real words, nonsense words, individual letters and numbers (for example, Murray, 1966; Engle, 1974; Penney, 1979).

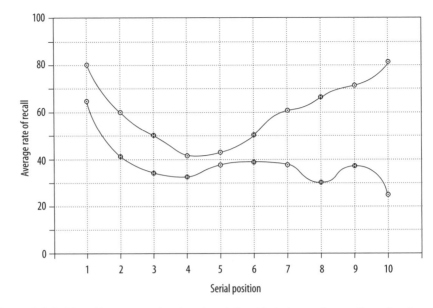

Figure 2.4 Serial position curves, showing the relationship between the position of an item in a spoken string and the likelihood of its being recalled correctly (after Postman and Phillips, 1965).

If the likelihood of an item being recalled is plotted against its position within a string, the resulting graph is known as a Serial Position Curve. The upper of the two curves in Figure 2.4 shows a typical pattern for immediate recall of a 10-item string. The initial few positions, in which recall is relatively high, are known as the *primacy* portion of the curve. The final few positions, in which recall is also relatively high, are known as the *recency* portion of the curve. The improved recall of the items in the last few serial positions is known as the *recency effect*.

Research has shown that the amount of material recalled is roughly constant no matter how long the string (Miller, 1956). If longer strings are presented, the number of items recalled from the early part of the string and the latter part of the string will remain largely unchanged, but far more items in the middle of the string will be forgotten. For example, Postman and Phillips (1965) presented subjects with lists of 10, 20 or 30 words and measured recall. They obtained the upper curve shown in Figure 2.4 for the 10-word lists, while for the 20- and 30-word lists they obtained curves that showed similar primacy and recency portions but had deeper and more prolonged troughs in the middle.

In addition to comparing the effects of different lengths of string, Postman and Phillips also examined the effect of introducing a delay before asking subjects to recall what they had heard. On some trials, subjects were asked to perform a distracter task for thirty seconds after hearing the string, then recall as much of the string as possible. Under these conditions, subjects still recalled the first few items well, but recall of the last few items declined significantly. The results are shown as the lower curve in Figure 2.4. It can be seen that the recency effect is entirely absent: the recall rate drops after the primacy portion of the curve and then stays low throughout the string. The same effect was noted for the 20- and 30-word lists.

This finding has led researchers to speculate that human beings possess a short-term auditory memory that can store incoming sound in its raw form for short periods. According to this hypothesis, the last few items of a speech string will be recalled more accurately than the earlier items because they are still held in the short-term auditory store. However, if subjects are prevented from accessing this store immediately, as is the case when they are asked to carry out a distracter task, the trace fades or is overwritten with new material and the last few items cannot be recalled any better than the earlier items.

The exact nature of the store is still a matter of debate, as is its capacity, which has been variously reckoned by researchers to be as little as 1.5 seconds and as much as 20 seconds or even more. In spite of disagreements over the details, however, the evidence that such a store exists is strong (one such model is the Precategorical Audio Store or PAS proposed by Crowder and Morton, 1969).

2.4.2 The Modality Effect

An interesting feature of the recency effect is that it works for visually presented lists as well as for spoken lists. It has been suggested that this is because people usually articulate words silently (sub-vocalization) during reading, and that this helps in word recognition. This view is supported by research findings that show that words which sound alike are more likely to be confused than words which look alike, regardless of whether the material is presented visually or aurally (Conrad, 1964; Baddeley, 1966).

However, while the recency effect is apparent both for visual and auditory presentation, it is far more pronounced during auditory presentation. Research has shown that if subjects are asked to memorize seven or eight digits presented either visually or through speech, retention of the first few digits will be more-or-less the same in both cases, but retention of the last few digits will be stronger in those who receive the auditory presentation (Penney, 1975). This is known as the modality effect. It can be regarded as something that enhances the recency effect.

The number of items affected varies from experiment to experiment, but almost all studies have shown greater recall of at least the last three digits presented, while Murray (1966) found improvements on up to five digits. The effect has been tested in conjunction with a Peterson distracter task (in which subjects are given three letters or words to recall, then asked to count down from a given number in increments of three until asked to stop and recall the letters or words) and the superiority of auditory over visual presentation was still apparent, provided the distracter did not require a long period of vocalization (Penney, 1989).

The modality effect can also be seen to operate on a subject's own vocalization. Thus, a subject receiving a visual stimulus can improve short-term retention by overtly vocalizing the stimulus while reading it. However, while this works as well as external auditory presentation for the most recently acquired items, it tends to reduce recall of earlier items in the list.

2.4.3 The Auditory Suffix Effect

The auditory suffix effect was identified by Conrad (1960) and has since been investigated by a number of other workers (for example, Dallett, 1965; Crowder, 1967). It is the effect whereby recall of a list of spoken items (such as a sequence of digits) is impaired if a further sound is added to the end of the list. Thus when Conrad gave his subjects a list of items and then issued the instruction "Recall", their performance was impaired compared with the condition in which the instruction to recall was given through non-auditory means.

Like the modality effect, the auditory suffix effect operates on the most recently stored items in a list and has little effect on the retention of items appearing earlier in the list. It can therefore be viewed as an effect that interferes with the operation of the recency effect.

The auditory suffix effect exists for both speech and non-speech sounds but is very much greater for speech. Crowder and Morton (1969) explored the effect extensively and found that presenting a non-speech sound such as a buzzer or tone immediately after a list of items had no significant effect on recall, but that any speech suffix would impair recall. The effect was apparent regardless of whether the spoken suffix was meaningful or recognizable or simply a nonsense word.

Ayres et al. (1979) investigated the role of speech in triggering the effect. They gave subjects a serial recall task followed by either a spoken syllable or a musical sound. The sounds were all easily distinguishable from one another, with the exception of the sound "wa" which was deliberately structured so that it could be heard either as a spoken syllable or as the sound of a musical instrument. This sound was then presented both among the musical sounds and among the speech sounds. The results indicated that the speech suffixes, including the "wa" sound, disrupted recall far more than did the musical suffixes, but that when the "wa" sound was perceived as a musical instrument it had far less disruptive effect than when it was perceived as an item of speech.

2.4.4 Summary

The research described above suggests that human beings have a short term audio memory with a more-or-less fixed-length of a few seconds, that we are best at remembering the first few items in a string and the last few (the recency effect), and that we are more likely to remember the last few items if they are followed by silence rather than by further items of speech (the auditory suffix effect).

These findings have a number of implications for the design of speech strings. They suggest that all such strings should be kept very short and followed by a silent pause, allowing the listener time to process information out of the short-term auditory store and into some more durable form before accepting new information. The research also suggests that it would be beneficial if the important information in a speech string is placed towards the end, immediately preceding a period of silence.

The findings further suggest that speech may not be the best medium to use in all cases. The research on the auditory suffix effect suggests that most non-speech sounds do not occupy as much space in short-term memory as speech, and that non-speech sounds also cause less disruption to other cognitive processes. Thus there may be occasions on which it would be better to use non-speech tones instead of speech.

2.5 Meaning: More than Semantics

There is a considerable body of linguistic and psycholinguistic research concerned with language processing and the mechanisms by which people extract meaning from language, but much of this work is concerned with language generally rather than with spoken language. Even when speech has been the focus of research, the emphasis has usually remained on the relationship between structure and received meaning, and there is little to guide the designer who wishes to move in the opposite direction – to start with a message and identify the most appropriate structure through which to convey that message.

An exception to this may be found in the work of Paul Grice (1975). A philosopher rather than a linguist, Grice was interested in the process by which human beings deal with apparent ambiguities in speech. He noted that a given sentence might, without changing form in any way, serve several very different purposes, and he argued from this that meaning is dependent upon context as well as content. His approach, offered as an alternative to the structural theories of the time, has come to be known as the Pragmatic Theory.

Grice argued that the meaning of a sentence is dependent not only on its internal semantic content but also on a set of assumptions currently held by both the speaker and the listener at any given point in a discourse. Thus, a sentence which may appear ambiguous or even logically inconsistent in isolation may make perfect sense within a conversation, provided both speaker and listener share the same assumptions about its role within the current discourse. This allows a wide range of forms to be used in spoken language, increasing the possibilities for economy of words and expressive power. However, if the speaker makes an incorrect judgement regarding the listener's current assumptions and formulates a sentence on this basis, the listener may receive the wrong meaning or no meaning at all. In this case the conversation will founder until the two participants have re-established the common ground necessary for mutual understanding.

On this basis, Grice argued that conversation is essentially a cooperative process. He suggested that at any point in a conversation a speaker should be guided by what he called the Cooperative Principle (CP), which he defined as:

> Make your conversational contribution such as is required, at the stage at which it occurs, by the accepted purpose or direction of the talk exchange in which you are engaged. (Grice, 1975, p. 45)

This is a very general principle, as Grice himself realized. He therefore proposed a series of sub-maxims that he regarded as following logically from the Cooperative Principle. He grouped these sub-maxims under four headings.

1. *Quality*   say only what is true and what you know to be true
2. *Quantity*   say no more and no less than is required
3. *Relation*   be relevant
4. *Manner*   be perspicuous (be brief and orderly; avoid obscurity and ambiguity)

These guidelines, although very general, do form a useful starting point for anyone addressing the problem of dialogue design. Some, such as the need to provide truthful answers, appear to be quite easy to apply, but others clearly need to be expanded and made much more specific before they can be applied in practice. We will look at some of the ways in which this might be done in the following chapters.

2.6 Effects of Speech Quality

Research shows that poor pronunciation and other forms of degradation significantly increase the effort involved in assimilating speech and the likelihood that items will be misunderstood.

Nusbaum and Pisoni (1985) noted that listeners faced with poor-quality speech are forced to rely heavily on the semantic content of the speech in order to resolve ambiguities. They suggested that this could be used as a means to measure the intelligibility of synthetic speech systems. They asked subjects to listen to a number of sentences, some of which were grammatically correct and meaningful while others had the syntactic structure of English sentences but made no sense. They found that when the sentences were presented using natural speech there was only a small difference between the recognition accuracy obtained on the meaningful sentences (99.2%) and on the nonsense ones (97.7%, a drop of 1.5%). However, when the sentences were presented using various speech-synthesis systems, the recognition rate obtained on the nonsense sentences was significantly lower than that obtained on the meaningful sentences (down from 90.7% on average to 76.3%, a drop of 14.4%). On the basis of these findings, Nusbaum and Pisoni argue that much synthetic-speech is of relatively poor quality and that listeners have to perform additional semantic analysis in order to reduce or resolve ambiguities. Thus the synthetic speech demands greater effort from the listener.

There is also evidence that poor speech quality makes additional demands upon the short-term memory. Posner and Rossman (1965) hypothesized that speech processing is in competition with other mental processes for limited memory resources, and that an increase in the demands made by the speech-processing task (for example, because the speech is degraded) might therefore be expected to reduce the efficiency with which other tasks are performed. Luce and colleagues (1983) tested this proposition in a series of experiments that compared task performance using information presented either through natural or synthetic speech. They found that when subjects were asked to recall a series of digits in any order, there was little difference in performance between synthetic and natural speech presentation. However, when subjects were asked to recall digits in the order in which they were presented, performance was significantly worse for the synthetic speech condition. Luce et al. argue that this is because the latter task is significantly more difficult and places increased demand on short-term memory.

Luce (1982) presented subjects with passages of fluent connected speech generated either by a human speaker or a speech-synthesizer. He found that subjects presented with the natural speech were better able to answer questions on the semantic content of the message, whereas subjects presented with synthetic speech were better able to answer questions about the syntax and surface structure. He suggested that this might be because the synthetic speech made greater demands on the speech-processing system, and that, having put more time and effort into analyzing surface features, the subjects presented with synthetic speech would therefore be more aware of such features.

These findings suggest that even when synthetic speech is intelligible, it may impose far higher mental demands on the listener than natural speech. This is undesirable in all cases, but has particular implications where users may be carrying out demanding activities while listening to synthetic speech or listening to it for long periods. For example, a device that uses synthetic speech to allow "hands free" operation by motorists might prove dangerous if users have to concentrate so hard on deciphering the speech that they have little concentration left for driving. Similarly, a blind person using a speech-equipped computer may be at a considerable disadvantage compared with sighted users if deciphering the speech requires so much concentration that it leaves little for the task in hand.

In order to minimize such problems, designers should aim to make synthetic speech as much like natural speech as possible. This involves careful consideration of all aspects of the speech, including the quality of the individual phonemes, word-choice, sentence structure, pausing and rhythm, and intonation.

2.7 Summary and Conclusions

This chapter has reviewed some of the research and knowledge regarding the verbal and non-verbal content of natural speech. This information is important in designing machine-generated utterances from two points of view. First it is vital to recognize where there are non-verbal messages being carried in speech. Secondly, the chosen speech technology may or may not be able to support the non-verbal component. For instance, if a text-to-speech system allows only imprecise control of pitch it may be necessary to compose a question in the "wh" form rather than relying on an interrogative intonation pattern to signal the question.

Rhythm is a good example of a component of speech that comes naturally to good orators. Most people are only likely to recognize its contribution when done badly, perhaps by a non-native speaker. Application of the kind of "musical" analysis that has been described – in assembly and timing of synthesized utterances – could lead to much more natural and comprehensible utterances.

Analysis of intonation shows that a tone group may consist of a simple tonic segment containing the important information, and we have seen that importance depends on how new the information is in the context of the current dialogue. For instance, if the listener can see that the speaker has just looked out the window, then the speaker might simply say, "It's raining." That is new information, it was not known to the listener before. However, in another situation the speaker might say, "Look out the window, it's raining." The important information is still the same, the state of the weather, so that remains as the tonic, but a pretonic segment has been added with secondary information.

The auditory suffix effect is a vital consideration in designing speech utterances. A practical example is in directory assistance systems. A number announced thus: "The number you require is 01904 430000. Thank you for calling", is much more likely to be forgotten than one given without the polite but distracting suffix.

The discussion in this chapter has concerned natural spoken dialogue between two human participants. Such dialogue is a cooperative activity, in that the participants usually share the goal of achieving mutual understanding.[1] Thus when a person is speaking they are trying to do so in the way that the listener will best understand. For instance, the speaker will make judgements as to what information will be new to the listener, and will present that information appropriately according to the kind of rules outlined above. The human speaker will also instinctively know when it is appropriate to pause to allow time for the information to "sink in". Human dialogue is also interactive, so if the speaker makes incorrect assumptions (such as assuming that information is new when it is not) this will become apparent within the dialogue and the participants will attempt to repair the error.

The systems that are the subject of this book include as speakers not just humans but also machines. Most of these assumptions about the dialogue are no longer true. The objective of the machine's designer will be to impart unambiguous, intelligible information and so it is up to the designer to embody that in the design of the system and the utterances it will make, according to the kinds of rules outlined in this chapter.

This chapter has highlighted some of these considerations. In subsequent chapters we will see how these can be put into practice in designs.

Further Reading

The role of pausing in speech:
Goldman-Eisler (1972)
Grosjean and Deschamps (1973)
Duez (1972)

Evidence for a short-term auditory store:
Darwin, Turvey and Crowder (1972)
Glucksberg and Cowan (1970)
Cowan, Litchi and Grove (1988)
Moray, Bates and Barnett (1965)

---

[1] This may not be true in extreme cases. For instance, if a police officer is interrogating a suspect, the objective of the suspect may well be to steer the officer away from the truth. As another example, humour often relies on a speaker mis-leading the listener as to the true direction of the conversation; there is no joke if the listener guesses the punch-line before it has been given.

Interaction Design

Having considered the linguistic factors underlying good speech communication, we move on to consider how this knowledge can be applied in practice. The design of speech-based devices can be broken down into two stages: Interaction Design (i.e. what information should be communicated, and when) and Dialogue Design (i.e. how the required information should be communicated). These two stages are not completely distinct from one another, but separating them allows the arguments to be developed more clearly. This chapter covers the first stage, Interaction Design.

3.1 Differences Between Visual and Auditory Interfaces

To design a good speech-based interface the designer has to be aware of the elements of psychology outlined in Chapter 2. Phenomena such as primacy and recency are not common knowledge nor intuitive. This contrasts to some extent with the situation of the designer of a visual interface. It might be argued that the designer of such an interface ought to know about visual perception and psychology, but in practice a lot of that knowledge is to hand, in the form of the designer's experience and intuition – as well as in more tangible forms such as design guidelines. It is a major objective of this book to provide designers with corresponding guidelines and intuition as to how best to design speech-based interfaces.

The fundamental difference between a speech-based interface and a visual one is in the amount of information that can be presented. Writers sometimes (loosely) refer to the difference in bandwidth between the visual and the auditory channel. That is to say that it is possible to present a lot of information at any time in a visual form. Strictly speaking, vision does not process this in parallel, but we have good control of our sight and can switch focus between areas quickly and easily. By contrast, hearing is less focused and more serial in nature.

In the design of any visually based interface, it is easy for the designer to add new features. For instance, if it is decided that some new piece of information should be available, another indicator can be added to the display. The user can be expected to cope with such additions unless and until the display become excessively cluttered. When this new indicator changes then the user's attention will be drawn to it and they will automatically shift their focus from whatever they were looking at before to the new item. This combination of catching attention (often in the peripheral area of vision) and shifting focus means that we can process visual information almost in parallel.

Regardless of what some people assert, hearing is not a strictly serial medium. One only needs to examine an every-day task such as driving to illustrate this.[1] The driver may be having a conversation with the passenger, yet at the same time be aware of what is on the radio. He will use the engine note as an indication as to when to change gear. At the same time he will be able to pick up sounds indicating special conditions, such as a rumble suggesting a problem with the engine or the siren of an approaching ambulance. The ability to monitor different sources of sound depends very much on the phenomenon of *auditory streaming*, which is discussed further in Chapter 8. The mechanisms by which auditory attention can be shifted and the degree to which it can be refocused are very different from their visual counterparts. One of the implications is that the designer must think very hard before adding another auditory indicator to a display.

3.2 User Selection versus Designer Direction

The greatest advance in the usability of computers is due to the graphical user interface (GUI). There are a number of aspects of such interfaces that make them easier to use, quite aside from their attractive appearance (there are many books on the design of GUIs, but Tognazzini (1992) gives a good insight into some of the more general aspects).

A traditional computer interface prompts the user when it is ready to receive a command. The user may enter any command. Depending on the state of the system some commands may be invalid, in which case

---

[1] The driving example is used in Buxton (1989).

the system will respond with an error message. In other words, the user is allowed to make mistakes – and is admonished when they do. GUIs exploit the dynamic properties of the graphical display in such a way as to reduce the number of errors a user can commit. In other words, it is generally not possible to enter a command when it would be invalid. A common mechanism to enforce this is the "greying-out" of menu entries. When the user pulls down a menu, any entries within it that are not currently valid are displayed in a grey typeface. This is an immediate indication to the user that that entry is invalid, but furthermore the entry cannot be selected. In this way the user is protected from mistakes – and from error messages.

An alternative would be to remove invalid items from menus. They would be similarly inaccessible, but the menus would appear to be inconsistent. What is normally the sixth item in the menu might become the fourth when two of its predecessors are inaccessible. Their sudden disappearance might confuse users who would puzzle as to their absence, whereas a greyed-out item has evidently been invalidated for a reason. There is minimal overhead for the user in pulling down a menu, scanning its entries and noticing that one or more of them is greyed out.

This is not true for a speech-based menu. The time taken to listen to a list of menu entries – many of which may turn out to be inaccessible anyway – may be a significant waste.

It is thus very important that the designer of a speech-based system:

(a) Limits the number of choices available at each stage of the interaction to an absolute minimum;

(b) Keeps each item as short as possible;

(c) Tries to anticipate what the user is most likely to need at each stage of the interaction and presents that information first.

In other words, the designer of a speech-based system should follow Grice's maxims (discussed in Chapter 2), and aim to make speech outputs brief and relevant.

3.3 Determining Relevance

Keeping spoken items as brief as possible is relatively straightforward (and we will look at the mechanics of this in the next chapter). However, being relevant – i.e. limiting choices to a minimum while still providing what the user is most likely to need at a particular stage in an interaction – is far more difficult.

In some situations it is more-or-less impossible to predict what option or information the user will require next. For example, if the user of a computer system finishes a task and quits the program they have been using, how can a system designer predict what they will do next? They might shut down the computer, or else start a new task using any of the other programs available.

In such situations, attempting to make predictions is of limited value. In the case of a system that is always used by the same person (or a limited number of regular users) it may be possible to gather statistics on usage and tailor the system responses accordingly. However, in most situations this is simply not possible. The best the designer can do is to present a list of the choices available in as accessible a manner as possible. The problems posed by menus, lists, etc., will be looked at in more detail in Chapter 6.

However, even when there appears to be only one possible response, it is not always easy to ensure that the response is relevant. Much of the information presented by interactive systems is relevant in the general sense that it is a response to a user action and it relates to that action. However, much of it may not be relevant in the more specific sense defined by Grice, i.e. that it is what the user is expecting at that point in the discourse. Interactive systems often generate a great deal of information that is only indirectly related to the user action or system change which prompted the response.

For example, consider an in-car guidance system. When asked to indicate the current position of the car, the guidance system might respond with a message such as:

> You are near M1 junction 12, southbound

This is clearly a valid response to such a request. However, not all of the information presented may be relevant to the driver. For example, a driver who has been travelling along the same road for some time will almost certainly know what road it is, and in which direction he or she is travelling. Therefore, only the junction number is strictly relevant. However, a driver who has only recently turned onto the road might welcome confirmation that the correct turn has been taken.

How can we determine what is relevant in circumstances like this? As a first step we might ask ourselves: can the response be broken down into two or more shorter responses, each of which is a response to a separate question?

In the case of the example above it is quite easy to see that this can be done. One part of the output is a response to the question "Which road am I on?" while the other is a response to the question "Whereabouts on this road am I?". We could therefore break-up the response into two separate responses, each of which is a relevant answer to one of these questions.

Of course, reducing responses to the bare minimum in this way may mean that the user has to issue more requests in order to obtain information. However, there is no reason why the system could not be programmed to keep track of the interaction and use a simple model to predict what the user may require next. For example, when the in-car guidance system is asked for an update on the car's position, it might check its records and discover that the last message was issued only a few minutes ago and included the information that the car is heading south on the M1. Therefore, its model might predict that the driver does not need to hear this information again and only needs to know the number of the last junction passed. On the other hand, if the driver has recently exited at a junction, the model might predict that the driver needs much more information.

How accurate it is feasible to make such a model is difficult to say. For instance, a particular user may have a memory problem and need to be reminded which road he or she is on every five minutes. That would imply the need for individual user models and for feedback mechanisms whereby the model could learn more about the user. Ultimately this kind of model is part of the much broader research topic of Natural Language Processing (NLP).

Compare this with the task facing the designer of a visual interface, who will almost certainly not try to decide what is relevant (nor allow the software to decide) but instead present "all" the information and leave the user to decide which bits are relevant. The user of such a visual guidance system would soon learn that (for example) the top line of the display always contains the current road and direction, and would only look at it when that was the information required.

The designer of an interface may be able to control relevance to some extent by managing the interaction. For example, instead of presenting the whole range of options to the user at once, the system might lead the user through a hierarchy of selections. Thus, instead of being presented with, say, 16 options, the user might be led through four menus each with four entries, controlling the relevance and narrowing the focus with each selection.

A practical limiting factor is human memory capacity for speech strings. If a response is short enough to be held in memory while the user ponders and reacts to it, there is little point in making it shorter still.

As we saw in Chapter 2, the research evidence suggests that we can hold around 2–20 seconds worth of "raw" speech. By raw we mean complete speech strings with pauses, hesitations, intonation, etc. However, the amount of relevant information a speech contains may be quite low – a five-second speech may contain just one word of information that is "new" to a listener, or perhaps just one or two numbers. Therefore the length of the short-term auditory memory is not necessarily a good guide to how much information we can store.

Another approach is to define an upper limit for the number of digits, words, individual letters, etc., that can be held in memory. Numerous psychologists have studied this issue, and some of the research in this area was discussed in Chapter 2. In particular, it has been noted that human beings appear to possess a memory store that has a more-or-less fixed capacity for numbers, individual letters, and similar items of information. It is this fixed-capacity store which is assumed to give rise to the auditory suffix effect, whereby someone who is already holding a number of items in memory is presented with a further item and is only able to store it by forgetting one of the earlier items.

Miller (1956) reviewed much of this research and reached the now-famous conclusion that the human short-term memory store can hold approximately seven items of information ("7 plus or minus 2"). However, this does not mean that the upper storage limit is 7 ± 2 individual digits, words, or whatever. Rather, it is *7 ± 2 items of information*, and each of those items might be a single digit, a group of digits, a letter, a word, or a phrase. The determining factor is that the item, or group of items, is recognized by the listener as a single piece of information. Hence a significant date such as 1066 might be recalled as a single item of information, even though it comprises four digits. Similarly, a name or phrase that is familiar to the listener might constitute a single item of information, even if it contains many individual words.

To use a computing analogy, we might envisage human short-term memory as a 5–9 element array that can store either an integer, a character, a string or a pointer in each element. The pointers would reference items in long-term memory. If a phrase or number is unfamiliar to the listener it will be stored in the array as individual strings, integers, etc., thus occupying many elements. However, if a word, phrase or number is already familiar to the listener, all that has to be stored in the array is a single pointer to the corresponding item in long-term memory.

Because of the way in which human short-term memory works, it is very difficult to gauge how much spoken information the user of a speech-based system will be able to recall at any one time. Since it depends in large part on how familiar the items of information are, a particular spoken response may prove more difficult for one individual to store than another. However, there are a number of guidelines we can apply for certain types of information – such as numbers – and we will look at some of these in Chapter 4.

To summarize, we can assess the relevance of our responses by asking ourselves:

● can the intended response be broken down into two or more shorter responses, each of which is a response to a separate user input?

● can the response be held in memory while the user ponders and reacts to it?

These guidelines can be applied to most responses generated by interactive systems, and we will look at some practical examples in later chapters.

Unfortunately, this approach does not adequately deal with commands that produce list-like responses, such as requests for a list of the files in a directory. Some of the information produced by such commands can be regarded as responses to separate, specific questions. For example, if a directory-listing command automatically provides information on file-sizes or disk-usage, we could remove this information and provide it only in response to specific requests. However, even if such information is removed we may still be left with a lengthy list of file data which is apparently all of one kind and which cannot be presented briefly. Such commands will have to be dealt with in another way, and this issue is addressed in Chapter 6.

3.4 The Role of Expectation

As Grice pointed out, speech communication depends for its efficiency on the participants having a shared context. As a result, it is reasonable to assume that each participant will have certain expectations as to what might – or could – be said next at each stage within a dialogue.

For example, if we say to a friend "Have you been busy today?", we have certain expectations as to what the response will be. Even though the range of valid responses to such a question is very large, we might reasonably expect a response that can be broadly categorized as "yes", "no" or somewhere in between. Therefore, if the answer is "Not too bad" or "It was frantic this morning" or "Wednesdays are always slow", we will quickly be able to categorize the answer and move on to the next stage of the dialogue. However, if the response is "That chap from Marketing came around this afternoon…" we may feel a little perplexed. We will either have to wait and hope that the relevance of this statement becomes clear in the next sentence or two, or stop the speaker and ask for clarification.

Holding such expectations enables us to take part in relatively complex spoken exchanges without excessive mental effort. Where expectations are met, we can deal with a response with the minimum of analysis and effort. However, when our expectations are not met we will be forced to re-evaluate our possible responses. Thus the communication will be slower or may even break down entirely.

The precise expectations we have about a particular response will be shaped by various factors. The main factor will be the question or statement that gave rise to the response, but underlying this will be other factors such as the following.

- The listener's knowledge of the speaker, and of his/her use of language. For example, unless the speaker is a very young child or someone who does not have English as a first language, the listener will probably expect responses to conform to basic grammatical rules, and will thus have certain expectations regarding sentence structure, etc.

- The content and nature of the discourse prior to this exchange. For example, the subject of an exchange may already have been mentioned, in which case a speaker might use, say, a pronoun instead of a noun (e.g. "he" or "she" instead of a person's name). This would avoid repetition and might also shorten a response. However, it would only be a valid response if the listener is expecting to hear a pronoun at this point in the exchange and knows who or what it signifies.

- The situation in which the discourse takes place. For example, the language used when chatting with friends in a pub may be quite informal, containing a high percentage of minor sentences (see Section 4.4) and possibly including the use of slang terms. By contrast, the language used during a job interview is more likely to be formal, placing far greater reliance on major sentences and involving few if any slang terms.

- The backgrounds, concerns, beliefs, etc., of those participating, and the extent to which these are shared. For example a British English speaker might "translate" some words and phrases when talking to an American. "Secondary school" might become "high school", "motor-way" "freeway" and so on.

Much of this also applies when spoken interaction takes place between a human being and a machine, rather than between two or more human beings. Again, the main factor will be the question or statement that gave rise to the response, but other factors might include:

- The listener's knowledge of the system, and its use of language. For example, unless the system is known to be particularly terse or verbose in its responses (or to have been written by programmers with a poor grasp of English), the listener will probably expect responses to conform to basic grammatical rules, and will thus have certain expectations regarding sentence structure, etc. The user may also have specific knowledge of a system and know, for example, that the error messages it produces usually take a particular form. Given that interactive systems are generally much more limited in their range of responses than human beings, a regular user may be able to predict the form of a system's responses with considerable accuracy.

- The content and nature of the interaction prior to this exchange. For example, the name of a file that failed to print may already have been mentioned, in which case a response might refer to it indirectly (e.g. as "it") rather than by name. However, this would only be valid response if the listener is expecting to hear "it" at this point in the exchange and knows what it signifies.

These factors cause us to have certain expectations regarding the structure and content of a response, and if these expectations are met, either wholly or in part, we will be able to process the responses easily and quickly.

There is some evidence that the prosody accompanying a piece of speech aids us in determining whether a response matches our expectations or not. We might assume that the principal factor is the semantic content of a speech, which is determined by thoroughly analyzing its lexical and syntactic content. According to some linguists, this is precisely how human speech perception works – a stream of speech is first parsed into individual words, then the meaning of each word is found by looking it up in a "mental lexicon", after which the meaning of the whole utterance is determined by analyzing the grammatical relationships between the words. This can be characterized as a "bottom-up" approach.

However, other linguists argue that we analyze speech using a "top-down" approach. According to this theory, we use prosodic cues (pausing, intonation, etc.) to help us locate the key words within the speech stream, then use these to reconstruct the remainder of the utterance. Only if the meaning cannot be recovered in this way do we resort to a full-blown lexical and syntactic analysis of the speech stream.

In short, we might not need to listen to all the words in a speech response to determine whether or not it matches our expectations; it might be sufficient to pick-out the key words, which will be easy if they are correctly highlighted through prosody. This view remains controversial, but even linguists who reject it generally agree that prosody plays an important role in speech perception.

Based upon the foregoing, the process of assimilating a spoken response from a speech-based device can be analyzed in the following way:

- At the outset, the user may know specifically what form the next response will take, or, more probably, will know that it can take one of a limited number of forms (for example, an indication of success or failure). If the syntactic and prosodic features of the response closely match the user's expectations, the response will be identified very rapidly and the user can move on.

- If the user is not able to predict the content of the response precisely (because it contains some element of new information), he or she may still know the general form the response will take and the probable nature of the new information. Thus the user may already know the purpose of the new information and needs only the information itself, perhaps just one or two words. This reduces or even removes the need to perform any syntactic analysis on the response. All that is required is to find the new information within the speech string, and this will be easy if the new information is marked by prosodic cues such as pitch prominence.

- Even if the user has no specific knowledge of the current system and the form of its responses, he or she will have certain expectations based upon knowledge of natural language. These include knowledge of the relationships between prosody, semantics and syntax, and of the frequency with which different language constructions are used. Using this knowledge, the user will attempt to identify the purpose of the response and the location of any critical information within it. Only if the response differs entirely from the user's expectations will it be necessary to perform full lexical and syntactic analysis.

It should be clear from this description that expectation plays a large part in determining how much effort is needed to extract meaning from a given speech string. Even when the user does not know exactly what response a system will produce, he or she will have certain expectations as to what is a relevant response and what is not. Provided these expectations are met – i.e. the response is relevant – the user will be able to process the response and move on with minimal effort.

It should also be clear that expectation concerns not just the content of the response but also its form. Our knowledge and experience of natural language leads us to expect that responses will conform to basic grammatical rules, and that they will be suitable for speech communication in terms of length, formality, vocabulary, etc. Thus the easiest responses to process will be those that use sentence structures widely found in speech; we will look at the differences between the structure of written and spoken sentences in the next chapter.

Recognition and assimilation will also be aided if all the cues are in accord with one another so that, for example, a word or phrase highlighted as "new" by the prosodic structure does indeed contain new information. This can be seen as providing a layer of redundancy. Conversely, unusual speech structures or ones in which the prosodic structure is at odds with the semantic content will be less expected and will contain less redundancy, forcing the listener to perform more analysis in order to extract the meaning and so making the interface more difficult to use.

3.5 Giving the Listener Control

Keeping speech-strings brief and relevant and ensuring that they match the listener's expectations as closely as possible will make a speech-based interface much more usable. However, there are times when even the best-designed interface will present the wrong information at the wrong time. Therefore it is essential that the user be given sufficient control to quickly steer the interaction back onto the right path.

This may be regarded as one of the most fundamental goals for the designer of a speech-based device – to ensure that information flow is, as far as possible, controlled by the user.

One of the most basic but important control functions is a "mute" facility. In many cases the user will be able to determine whether a response is the required one or not after hearing only part of the word or phrase. In such cases, it would be very slow and frustrating if the user were forced to listen to the whole of each word or phrase before moving on to the next or altering the flow of conversation in some way. Rather, it should be possible to reject an item at any time, no matter how little of it has been heard, and move immediately onto the next item. This is particularly important when scanning menus and lists – even short ones.

As well as being able to mute items, listeners should be able to demand that items be repeated or clarified if they were not heard or understood properly at first hearing. Providing a mute facility is fairly straightforward, but a repeat facility, if it is to be genuinely useful, requires careful design, and providing clarification is more difficult still.

As an example of how all this might be achieved, consider the DOStalk system (Pitt, 1996). DOStalk is a PC command-shell, based on DOS but designed for use by blind people and optimized for speech rather than visual output.

DOStalk is equipped with a number of "hot-keys" that provide control of the speech stream. We will look at each one in turn.

3.5.1 Mute Key

The action of this key is to mute any speech output immediately. Since the ability to mute speech quickly and easily is regarded as an important requirement of a good speech-based interface, the Mute key should be easily accessible. In DOStalk, which is designed to run on standard PCs, it was assigned to the space-bar, a large and easily found key. In a dedicated system a special key could be provided for this function, preferably a large and easily accessible one.

3.5.2 Repeat Key

This key causes the system to repeat the last item spoken, regardless of whether this was a response from a command, an error message, speech feedback resulting from a user action (e.g. typing), or a message produced as a result of pressing another control key (such as the More Information key – see below).

The Repeat facility can be invoked while a speech is in progress – there is no need to wait until the system has finished speaking. Like all the other speech output from the system, repeated messages can be muted using the Mute key.

An important issue which needs to be taken into account when designing a repeat facility is the problem posed by the "Brick Wall" effect. This problem has been identified by, among others, Yankelovitch et al. (1995), and refers to the situation in which a user fails to understand a message, but on attempting to obtain clarification is merely presented with the same message again. In these circumstances the user can quickly become very frustrated. Yankelovitch et al. suggest that this can reduce an individual's ability to think clearly and find ways around the obstacle. They suggest that this poses far more problems for the user of a speech-based interface than it does for the user of a visual interface.

In order to minimize this problem, Yankelovitch et al. suggest that the form of the message should be varied. Even when no more useful information is provided, changing the form of the message makes it less likely that the system will be perceived as unhelpful and unresponsive. This may be because changing the form of a message is a tactic people use in everyday conversation to get around obstacles created by inadequate or ambiguous information.

The Repeat key in DOStalk therefore varies its response when pressed several times in succession. At the first press, it simply repeats the previous message in its original form. With subsequent presses it repeats the same words but varies the intonation.

In the case of some frequently encountered messages, DOStalk provides several variants for use when the user asks to hear the message repeated. In such cases, the initial message follows the usual rules and is designed to be as brief and relevant as possible. Successive presses of the Repeat key produce responses that contain exactly the same information but sacrifice brevity in favour of different grammatical constructions.

3.5.3 More Information Key

This key is designed to provide clarification of the last item spoken or, where appropriate, more information concerning that item. The kind of information provided by this key might include details of the outcome of a successful operation, or the reason(s) for the failure of an unsuccessful operation.

Where a considerable amount of further information is available, it is provided through successive presses of the More Information key, with the earlier key presses providing information of a general or high-level nature while further key presses provide progressively greater detail. This accords with the principal of "information scoping" described by Yankelovitch (1994).

When there is no more information available and the More Information key is required to provide clarification only, it does this by varying the form of the message, in a similar fashion to the Repeat key.

The operation of the More Information key in DOStalk can be illustrated with reference to the COPY command. COPY is the DOS command used to copy one or more files from one location to another. It accepts up to two parameters. The first is mandatory and specifies the file or files to be copied. The second is optional and specifies the destination for the copy operation. If no destination parameter is supplied, the command will use the current directory as the destination (provided the files to be copied are not also in the current directory).

If COPY is called with a wildcard character, the command will list each file it finds which matches the specification. If only one file is specified, its name is not printed. On completion, COPY produces the message:

    <number> file(s) copied

The COPY command within DOStalk works in a very similar way to the standard DOS COPY command but differs in a few significant respects. When only one file is to be copied, the only possible outcomes are success or failure. Rather than using words to carry such simple information, DOStalk responds with a brief, non-speech tone sequence that is designed to convey either success or failure (see Chapter 4 for more information on the design of non-speech tones). Using non-speech tones allows the information to be conveyed quickly and with minimum disruption to the user.

If the operation was successful, pressing More Information will produce the message:

    <filename> copied to <destination>

If the operation was unsuccessful, COPY will return a non-speech tone indicating failure and, if appropriate, the message "System error". Pressing More Information will provide more information about the nature of the error.

When more than one file is being copied, DOStalk responds in exactly the same way as for a single file and (if successful) merely returns the non-speech tone sequence indicating success. If More Information is pressed in these circumstances, DOStalk will state the number of files copied, e.g.:

    <number> files copied

Successive presses of More Information will cause DOStalk to name the files copied one-by-one and, if the user continues to press More Information, to cycle through the list again and again. Prosody is used to signal the start and end of the list, and to give the listener an approximate idea of the length of the list and the position of the current item within it (see Chapter 6).

If an attempt to copy a group of files is unsuccessful, DOStalk will return a "failure" tone accompanied, where appropriate, by the phrase "System error". If some of the specified files were copied but not others, pressing More Information will elicit a message of the form "x out of y files copied", where x is the number of files successfully copied and y is the number of files that match the specification. Following this, each successive call for More Information will provide details of one of the files that could not be copied. These messages will take the form:

    couldn't copy <filename> to <destination>

If the user continues pressing the More Information key, the program will return to the start of the list of uncopied filenames and cycle through it again, using prosody in the same way as before to signal the start and end of the list and to give the listener an approximate idea of the length of the list and the position of the current item within it.

The operation of the More Information key is illustrated in Tables 3.1 and 3.2.

Table 3.1 The sequence of responses produced by the DOStalk COPY command as a result of a successful operation involving more than one file

Automatic response	Non-speech tone indicating success	
Requests for More Information	1	\<number\> files copied
	2	\<filename 1\> copied to \<destination 1\>
	3	\<filename 2\> copied to \<destination 2\>
	...	...
	n	\<filename n\> copied to \<destination n\>
	$n+1$	\<filename 1\> copied to \<destination 1\>
	$n+2$	\<filename 2\> copied to \<destination 2\>
	etc.	

Table 3.2 The sequence of responses produced by the DOStalk COPY command as a result of a partially successful operation involving more than one file

Automatic response	Non-speech tone indicating error + "System error" (where appropriate)	
Requests for More Information	1	x out of y files copied
	2	\<filename 1\> copied to \<destination 1\> OR Couldn't copy \<filename 1\> to \<destination 1\>
	3	\<filename 2\> copied to \<destination 2\> OR Couldn't copy \<filename 2\> to \<destination 2\>
	...	...
	n	\<filename n\> copied to \<destination n\> OR Couldn't copy \<filename n\> to \<destination n\>
	$n+1$	\<filename 1\> copied to \<destination 1\> OR Couldn't copy \<filename 1\> to \<destination 1\>
	$n+2$	\<filename 2\> copied to \<destination 2\> OR Couldn't copy \<filename 2\> to \<destination 2\>
	etc.	

3.6 Conclusions

It should be clear from the foregoing that there are significant differences between visual interaction and speech-based interaction. In a visual interface, the designer makes a large amount of information available at any one time and the user makes a selection from it. In speech-based interaction, only one piece of information can be made available at a time, so the onus is on the designer to predict the user's requirements at each stage of the interaction as accurately as possible and provide just what is required.

Determining what the user needs to hear at each stage of the interaction – i.e. determining what is relevant – is very difficult. It was noted that speech communication is a cooperative activity in which shared assumptions allow each participant to determine what is relevant to the other. Central to these ideas is the notion of expectation – what does the listener expect to hear next given what has gone before? It may be possible to store a history of an interaction and use this information to determine what information – and hence assumptions – might be shared between the participants.

However, in order to make a response relevant we must ensure that while it contains all the required information, it does not contain unnecessary information. This, too, may be difficult to judge, but we can set some limits by ensuring that responses contain only one item of new information, and by taking into account human memory span.

Finally, the designer must recognize that no matter how well a speech-based system is designed, there will be times when communication breaks down. Therefore it is essential to provide mechanisms that allow the user to obtain clarification.

Dialogue Design

4

Once we have determined what is to be communicated, we must decide how to communicate it. This chapter covers the second stage of the design process – Dialogue Design.

4.1 Choosing Speech or Non-speech Presentation

Having identified the relevant information that should be provided in response to a command, thought must be given to the form of the response. It has been suggested that a relevant response should ideally be no more than one tone group in length. However, there may be occasions when even this is an unnecessarily long response, and it may be better to use non-speech sound instead.

Consider, for example, the case of a command that terminates without providing any information, for example, the UNIX CD command. Since the user issued the command, he or she will be expecting that it will terminate at some point. Therefore the new information is not that the command has terminated, but that it terminated at a particular time. This can readily be signalled by a non-speech tone. Any further information, such as a spoken response like "Completed" or "Ready", would be redundant and would violate the principle of keeping all outputs as brief as possible.

This also applies where the possible outcomes of a command are very limited in number, for example, just success or failure. It would be possible to use words such as "Success" and "Failure" as responses, but it seems likely that users would soon learn to recognize the outcome from the first syllable and would not need to hear the rest of the word. By contrast, non-speech tones could convey the same information in a brief and non-distracting way.

4.2 Designing Non-speech Responses

This book is about the design of speech-based systems. Non-speech sounds also have a very important role in interactive systems, but it is far beyond the scope of this book to go into their use and design in detail. Nevertheless in this section we will provide some pointers as to where and how non-speech sounds can be used and integrated with speech utterances.

The range of non-speech sounds available is vast; just think of the variety of sounds in music. Furthermore, technology capable of generating a wide range of sounds is readily available; a sound card is a standard component of most computers. There is ample evidence that large amounts of information can be conveyed using non-speech sounds, provided they are well designed (see Bly, 1982; Buxton et al., 1991; Brewster, 1994; Gaver, 1997; Blattner et al., 1992).

A great deal of work has been done on the design of non-speech sounds for interaction, and two contrasting approaches have been developed. They are known as auditory icons and earcons.

A computer icon is a small picture that in some way resembles the entity that it represents (a computer disc, a document or whatever). An auditory icon is the auditory equivalent – a sound that has a more-or-less direct link to the item it represents. For example, a waste-bin might be represented by the sound of a piece of paper being screwed-up and thrown into a metal container. The advantage of auditory icons is that they should be easy to recognize and to associate with their meaning. The power of auditory icons has been demonstrated through an enhancement to the Macintosh Finder system (Gaver, 1989) and in a simulation of a complex process control system (Gaver et al., 1991).

Earcons are symbolic but structured. The assignment of meaning to sound is arbitrary, but once the listener has learned the sounds and the rules through which they are combined, a good level of recognition can be achieved (see Brewster et al., 1992; Brewster, 1994).

In practice there are many sounds that fall between the extremes of auditory icons and earcons, sounds that do not directly resemble the entity represented but nevertheless have properties that people easily associate with meanings. Examples are notes on a rising scale, which are associated with openings or beginnings, and notes on a falling scale that can be used to indicate something closing or finished. High-pitched sounds may denote success while deeper ones can imply failure.

Non-speech sounds have several advantages over speech. They can present information quickly. They do not interfere with speech processing. They can be attention grabbing. People differ in the extent to which they can learn to interpret complex non-speech sounds, so they can be used where the precise meaning is not critical, or where supporting identification information is available. Examples of the use of non-speech sounds in speech-based systems include:

- *To cue speech*   If a system is to make a spoken utterance after a period of silence, the listener should be warned of the fact. If the speech is not cued, the listener may not be prepared for it and may not hear the first few words.

- *To mark the end of an utterance*   It may be important to know when an utterance is complete, and there is no further speech to be expected. This can be done with a non-speech sound, thus avoiding suffix effects. As suggested above, a falling tone or tones is a natural form of end marker.

- *As an alarm*   Sounds can be designed which evoke different levels of urgency (Edworthy et al., 1989, 1991; Patterson, 1989).

- *To give rapid, summary information*   Earcons have been used to represent overviews of mathematical equations (Stevens, 1996), information about incoming email messages (Mukerjee, 1997) and complex hierarchies (Brewster et al., 1995).

- *To give routine messages*   It is sometimes necessary for a system to give frequent, identical messages. For instance it may regularly confirm its status and that status may not change often. Using speech, with the same phrase repeated frequently (e.g. "System running normally"), could become annoying. The speech could be replaced by a simple tone that would provide the same confirmation, but be less annoying. Since it is heard frequently, its meaning will soon be learned, and this could be reinforced by the tone being accompanied by speech the first time it is generated.

This is illustrated in a study by Pitt (Pitt and Edwards, 1996). In an attempt to find what makes a good speech-based interface, an interface was designed that was deliberately intended to be bad. Guidelines on good design were consciously broken. A program (a "Hangman" word game) was given to test participants and their reactions collected. One of the deliberate faults introduced was that the program's responses were verbose and repetitive. For instance, at the end of each utterance, the program cued the user for the next input ("Please enter a letter."), a cue that could easily have been replaced by a simple tone. As predicted, users indicated they would prefer less speech and some showed clear signs of annoyance (such as shouting at the program, "Shut up!" and "I don't want to hear that!").[1]

As implied by some of the examples above, speech and non-speech sounds can often be integrated in a mutually supportive manner. For instance, the potential problem of a user forgetting the meaning of a given non-speech sound may be overcome if there is an option for the user to ask for the meaning, which will be given in speech. This aids learning so that soon the user does not require the speech backup.

4.3 Designing Speech Segments

Having decided what is relevant information, and dealt with responses that are better presented as non-speech sounds, the remaining issue is to design the speech responses. The research discussed earlier offers a number of pointers as to how best to do this.

There are various modulations that speakers use in order to signal the prominence of different parts of an utterance (as discussed in Section 2.2). In designing an utterance, therefore, it is first necessary to determine the relative importance of its various components.

We have noted that tone groups are units of information, and that each tone group normally contains one item of information that the speaker judges will be new to the listener. The speaker will balance the relative importance of the items to be presented in an utterance, and assign them phonological weight according to their newness. Linguists have identified various categories of information, some of which clearly fall into either the new or given category while others are more marginal. There is still much debate over this issue. The following list

---

[1] In fairness, when asked, none of the participants said that they would want to have non-speech sounds used in the program. However, without a controlled test using non-speech sounds in place of redundant speech, one cannot say whether this was prejudice on the part of the participants against "noisy" programs.

includes most of the more widely accepted categories of new and given information.

New

New information may be either:

- information that has not previously been mentioned, and which the listener cannot be expected to deduce from the context; or
- information that has previously been mentioned, but which the speaker judges the listener will not recall without prompting.

New information can be further subdivided into:

- *Brand-new*   This is information which is assumed not to be known by the listener.
- *Unused-new*   This is assumed to be known by the listener, but not currently in his or her consciousness.
- *Inferred-new*   These are entities that the listener can deduce from items already discussed. For instance, in a discussion on the topic "buses", the item "driver" is inferable. That is to say that even though the concept "driver" has never been mentioned, the speaker can assume that the listener will infer that any mention of "driver" refers to a bus driver.

Given

Information that is not new is Given. It will be given less prominence than New information. Given information can be further categorized as follows:

- *Evoked*   Evoked information has already been mentioned in the discourse – or is salient within the context of the current subject. Evoked information is not generally given phonological prominence.

Evoked information can be further divided into:

- *Evoked-current*   This is information which has recently been introduced into the discourse and to which all new information is currently related.
- *Evoked-displaced*   This is information that was previously Evoked-current, but which has now been displaced by more recent Evoked-current information.

55

○ *Evoked-from-context*   These are entities which have already been mentioned in the discourse or which are highly salient within the context of the current subject.

● *Inferable*   Inferable information has not been mentioned within the current discourse, but it is reasonable for the speaker to assume that the listener knows or could deduce it from the context.

The existence of these categories implies that a speech-based system must maintain a history of its interactions, which can be the basis of a model (however simple) of the user. User modelling is discussed further in Section 8.3.

Furthermore, it should be evident that it is not possible to determine what is or is not new information solely from the syntax of the utterance. For example, in the sentence:

Janet lifted the box

The new information in this sentence might be either "Janet", "lifted" or "box", depending on the context. If it was a response to the question "Who lifted the box?" then the new information is "Janet". If the question was "What did she do to the box?", then the new information is "lifted", while if the question was "What did Janet lift?", then the new information is "the box".

4.4 Major and Minor Sentences

Any information that is not new must be given information. However, it may not be necessary to include all the available given information in a dialogue. While some may perform a valuable supporting role (suitably marked through position and intonation as given information), some may be unnecessary.

In the examples given above, it can be seen that the whole sentence is not needed in each case. For example, if the question was "What did Janet do?" then an appropriate answer might be "She lifted the box". The word "she" in this case is given information – it merely reflects the questioner's use of the name – and could be omitted. Thus the sentence would become "Lifted the box". Similarly, if the question is "Who lifted the box?" then everything except "Janet" is given information and could be omitted. Thus there may be scope for reducing the length of dialogues by omitting given information.

The abbreviated responses "Lifted the box" and "Janet" are minor sentences, while the longer sentences from which they are derived are examples of major sentences. A major sentence is one that has the full grammatical form appropriate to its type. Thus a statement that has a formal declarative structure can be said to be a major (or regular) sentence.

Minor (or irregular) sentences use abnormal patterns whose clauses cannot be analyzed into a sequence of clause elements. Irregular sentences are used far more extensively in spoken English than in written English (Crystal, 1988). The fact that written and spoken language are different is a point which cannot be over-stressed in this book. There is a temptation for designers to think in terms of written language and to compose utterances which are syntactically correct, "good" English. Yet, since they are going to be presented in an auditory form, they should follow the conventions of spoken language. Minor sentences are the most important manifestation of this phenomenon. They are widely used for:

- standard forms of social interaction, for example, hello; how do you do?
- aphorisms, for example, easy come, easy go; like father, like son
- abbreviated sentence forms, for example, mix well; wish you were here
- interjections, for example, hey; tut, tut; shhhhh
- exclamations, questions or commands, for example, nice day; taxi?

Minor sentences are invariably shorter than equivalent major sentences, but they convey the same information. Thus they can save time when presenting spoken information. Some minor sentences succeed in conveying meaning only because they are frequently used. Thus it does not matter that the sentence is grammatically incomplete since it only serves to remind the user of the already-known complete form. An example of this is the use of "How do" as a greeting.

Other minor sentences work by dispensing with information which it is assumed the listener will be able to recover from the context, for example, saying "Looks great!" to someone who has just returned from a trip to the hairdresser. In this case, it is not necessary to include the subject of the sentence ("Your hair…") in order to convey the meaning of the utterance, even though the resulting sentence is grammatically incomplete.

4.5 Example of Designing Utterances for an Interactive System

For an example of the presentation of new and given information through minor sentences, consider a speech-based GPS car navigation system. The system has devised a route to a chosen destination (York). One of the system's functions is to calculate an estimated time of arrival (ETA). The driver requests the current ETA, and the system responds

> ETA at York is 1335

This is a minor sentence; its major equivalent would be "Your ETA at York is 1335". The only new information in this utterance is the time (1335). However, the other information is not entirely redundant; it cues the driver to expect the information requested and allows him to correct any errors. For instance, he may have evoked the ETA query in error. In that sense ETA is not evoked information, and could be new. Similarly he may have mis-programmed the destination and be expecting the ETA in Leeds. Notice that the new, salient information is placed at the end of the utterance, where it is most likely that driver will remember it.

Within a short time the driver requests an ETA again. The destination (York) is now Evoked-current information: it has been mentioned recently and the driver has not changed it (i.e. updated the destination). Its salience is so low that it should probably be omitted from the next utterance. The driver may find it annoying to be told again something he already knows. It is impossible to infer whether a repetition of a recent command is an error – or a sign of anxiety, so it is probably worth repeating the words "ETA is" which will also act as a cue to the forthcoming information. Thus on this second invocation, the response should be

> ETA is 1334

A human speaker might signal that the time has changed by inserting the word "now", further emphasizing that the time information is new, and there is no reason why a mechanical system should not do that.

ETA is now 1334

Similarly, if no time had been made or lost this could be emphasized.

ETA is still 1335

These utterances are repetitive in that they all contain "ETA is". As an alternative, these words might be replaced by a non-speech sound. A tone or earcon might be used which would both warn that speech is about to be generated and identify that speech as containing an ETA. Structured families of earcons might be used (Brewster, 1994) so that the user will easily recognize that the forthcoming utterance will be a time, and that it is an ETA. The earcons relating to different times would be similar, but different, and the earcon cueing the presentation of the ETA would also have similarities to the one evoked when the ETA was requested.

4.6 Choice of Phrasing

The usual form for a statement in English is the declarative form, in which the subject is followed by the verb which in turn is followed by the object. For example:

The boy kicked the ball

This is an active sentence. This ordering of the clause elements is common not only in statements but in most other language constructions. Crystal (1988) notes that, among clauses which contain a subject, verb and object, the three elements will occur in this order in around 90% of cases.

However, it is also possible for the clause elements to be switched around so that what was the object becomes the subject, for example.

The ball was kicked by the boy

This is a passive sentence. Baddeley (1993) notes that there is a considerable body of evidence showing that passive sentences are processed more slowly than active sentences, both when presented in writing or as speech. However, while passive sentences are widely used in writing, they are rarely used in speech. Passive sentences are most widely used in newspapers and textbooks and in other documents in which objectivity and an impersonal tone are desirable (Crystal, 1988). These qualities are rarely required in speech, except perhaps in courts of law. Many people have identified passive sentences as perhaps the most common example of unnecessarily complex language usage. George Orwell recommended that a passive sentence should not be used where an active sentence could be used instead, and groups campaigning for the use of plain English have adopted his advice.

Unfortunately the case is not so clear-cut when considering speech to be generated by a machine. Some people are uncomfortable with an inanimate object making use of the personal pronoun, "I". This is by no means a universal objection, though, and much research is currently under way into "humanizing" computer interfaces, giving as complete an illusion as possible that the user is interacting with a person. It is thus perhaps a matter of taste as much as anything, whether a system should be designed to say "I cannot respond to that request" or "It is not possible to respond to that request".

Baddeley (1993) also identifies a considerable body of evidence suggesting that negative sentences take longer to process than positive sentences. Thus, to use the same example as before, the sentence:

> The boy kicked the ball

will be processed more rapidly than its negative equivalent:

> The boy did not kick the ball

As with passive sentences, therefore, it is advisable to avoid negative sentences wherever possible.

4.7 Avoiding Ambiguity

Ambiguity can lead to errors and so is clearly undesirable, but it has also been shown that ambiguous sentences are processed more slowly than unambiguous ones.

MacKay (1966) found that the phrase

> after taking the right turn at the junction ...

was processed more slowly by subjects than the phrase

> after taking the left turn at the junction ...

He concluded that this was because "left" is unambiguous in this context while "right" can mean either "correct" or "right-hand".

Ambiguity and expectation can have similar effects. Morton and Long (1976) found that the sentence

> he sat reading the book until it was time to go home for tea

was understood more slowly when "book" was replaced by "bill". This may be because "bill" is more ambiguous than "book" (it can signify a demand for money, a draft of a proposed law, or the beak of web-footed bird), but other studies suggest that ambiguities which produce improbable or surreal interpretations have little impact on processing time. Therefore it seems likely that "book" is understood faster because it is expected; upon hearing the phrase "reading the", we anticipate that the next word will be "book" or "newspaper" or "magazine" or something similar. The word "bill", although acceptable, is unexpected, and therefore slower to process.

In addition to the problems posed by individual words, there are also problems posed by logically ambiguous clauses or phrases. Johnson-Laird (1970) considers the problems encountered in extracting meaning from the two sentences

> every man loves some woman

and

> some woman is loved by every man

Here the ambiguity is one of meaning. Does the first sentence mean that every man loves the same woman, or that every man loves a different woman? Similarly in the second sentence, does "Some woman" refer to a single woman or to a number of women? This ambiguity exists because the phrase "Some woman" is capable of being interpreted in two different ways. Although "woman" is singular, "Some woman" can refer in a generic way to many women.

In choosing the wording of a clause, it is important to avoid introducing any ambiguity.

It is not easy to envisage a method by which ambiguities of the type discussed above can be avoided. However, it seems likely that many of the phrases that might give rise to such problems are of a metaphorical or poetic nature. The example quoted by Johnson-Laird is an aphorism,

61

a statement that is intended to convey some widely applicable or "universal" truth in a short, pithy statement. It is unlikely that such phrases will occur with any frequency in human-machine dialogues.

The best advice is to thoroughly test any planned utterances, to see whether other people spot ambiguities that the designer has missed. Ambiguity arises precisely because the designer has a clear idea in mind as to the meaning of the phrase and is unlikely to consider alternative interpretations. Ambiguities are most likely to be noticed by other people since they will not have preconceptions about the intended meaning.

The problem of ambiguous words is a little easier to deal with. Such words are likely to fall into one of three categories: words which have the same sound but different meanings (homophones), words which have more than one meaning, and words with alternative pronunciations. Abbreviations may also be open to multiple interpretations, so these should be considered too.

4.7.1 Homophones: Words which Sound Alike

This group includes words such as "pear", "pair" and "pare". These are all normally pronounced identically, and therefore are indistinguishable to a listener. The meaning of a clause including one of these words must be recovered from the context but, as we have noted, this will almost certainly increase the time it takes the listener to process and respond to the speech. Therefore it would be best if such words could be avoided wherever possible.

A short list of such words is included in Appendix A.

4.7.2 Words with More than One Meaning

This group includes words such as "bill", "file" and "lean". Each has more than one meaning, but there is no difference in pronunciation to indicate the change of meaning.

In many cases, each different meaning is also a different part of language, and therefore will be distinguished by syntactic as well as semantic changes in context. The word "lean", for example, can be used as an adjective to mean "having no superfluous fat" or as a verb (transitive or intransitive) to mean "adopt or be in or place in an inclined position". Adjectives and verbs are used quite differently in sentence construction, and this should provide additional clues as to which meaning is intended.

In other cases, however, there is no syntactic difference to help with identification. Although the word "bill" can be used as a verb when referring to a bill of charges (as in "You will be billed for the damage") it is more commonly used as a noun both to refer to a bill of charges and to a duck's bill. Hence the ambiguity – and the resulting increase in processing time – noted by MacKay.

Again, it would be best if such words could be avoided wherever possible. A short list is included in Appendix B.

4.7.3 Words with More than One Pronunciation

These words cause particular problems with text-to-speech systems. That is because their correct pronunciation can only be derived from their context, implying an understanding of the meaning of the current usage. Examples are given in Table 4.1.

An example can be found in the computer version of the game Hangman mentioned earlier. When adapted for blind users through the use of a screen-reader and speech-synthesizer, the phrase "You have eleven lives left" was pronounced so that "lives" rhymed with "gives", rather than "hives" as the context required. This caused some confusion to users on first hearing, the unexpected pronunciation being sufficient to slow comprehension considerably.

In some cases the change of pronunciation reflects a change of function. The first pronunciation of "use" shown in Table 4.1 indicates that the word is being employed as a verb, while the second indicates that it is being employed as a noun. Here the difference is reflected in a change in syntax as well as a change in pronunciation. The word "read", by contrast,

Table 4.1 Examples of words with alternative, context-dependent pronunciations

Spelling	Pronunciation – rhymes with	Example of use
read	reed	I will read the book.
	red	I read the book yesterday.
use	fuse	Use your discretion.
	loose	I have no use for it.
live	give	I live in the UK.
	hive	He was electrocuted because the wire was live.

is almost always a verb, and pronunciation is used to indicate tense. Here too the difference will be reflected in a change in syntax as well as a change in pronunciation, but since the word is being used as a verb in both cases the difference is not great. Hence the role of pronunciation to point up the difference is probably more important in this case.

It is also important to note that in some cases the rhythmic structure of a word alters along with the pronunciation. The word "minute", for example, takes the stress on the first syllable when it indicates a unit of time, but when it is used to mean "very small" it takes the stress on the second syllable.

Words like these present problems because current text-to-speech systems may not be able to identify the appropriate pronunciation. Well designed systems include rules which correct for different pronunciations of strings within words (for example, the "ough" in "plough" and "enough") but much more sophisticated rules would be needed to deal with a situation in which the same word can be pronounced in different ways according to its use within a sentence.

However, where a designer is able to specify pronunciation for all speech outputs rather than relying on generally applicable rules, the problem need not arise. Such would be the case if the system used recordings of human speech, rather than text-to-speech synthesis. There is no reason why such words should be avoided provided the interface designer ensures that they are pronounced correctly and that any rhythmic changes are handled in an appropriate manner. A short list of such words is included in Appendix C.

4.7.4 Abbreviations

The meaning of many abbreviations is not immediately apparent when they are rendered into speech. The names of the days of the week, for example, are frequently represented in computer systems as three-letter abbreviations, and while some are relatively easy to understand, others sound odd and distracting even when the user is expecting them. When Thursday is abbreviated to "thu", for example, it is reproduced through many speech synthesis systems as "fuh". This is clearly ambiguous. Some speech synthesizers attempt to avoid this problem by including common abbreviations in their exceptions dictionaries. Thus, "Thu" would be spoken as "Thursday". There are two problems with this approach, however. The first is that there are circumstances in which the listener might need to know that a word is written in abbreviated form, but this will not be apparent if the system automatically expands it. Secondly abbreviations can be ambiguous; for example, Regent St. might be pronounced as "Regent Saint".

In general it is probably best to avoid any use of abbreviations. However, there may be some cases in which an abbreviated form is so widely used in colloquial English that it presents no problems. The use of "approx" as an abbreviation for "approximately" is one such case. In this case, using the abbreviation saves time without introducing ambiguity.

4.8 Personality

Until recently, speech has been an exclusively human activity. It is thus invested with many characteristics associated with human relationships. Now that we have machines that can speak, there are various conventions and associations that inevitably carry across from natural speech that we must be aware of.

In discussing some of these issues in this section, the reader should be aware that we are taking a certain position – one with which some people will not agree. For instance, we take the view that machines lack self-consciousness. That is to say that they cannot have a social or personal relationship to people. While it may be possible to provide a social façade or even to embody a simple model of social relations and adjust behaviour accordingly, there cannot be a relationship equivalent to a human–human one. That is our stance. There are those, some from the field of artificial intelligence, who would dispute this, who suggest that in time humans and computers will form relationships – and even that computers may become our social superiors.

Also, social relationships take place in a social environment. That environment will be different in different places. In particular, this writing is influenced by the environment of the UK and Ireland which is different from that in other counties. However, even if the details are different, the essential arguments remain true in any environment.

4.8.1 Politeness

In human dialogue the words we choose and the way we say them carries a lot of information about our attitude to each other. In particular we choose a level of politeness as an important social signal. That may mean that we say more words than are required in order to express social conventions. Contrast:

> Pass me the salt.

> Please pass me the salt.

and

> Would you mind passing me the salt, please?

It is beyond the scope of this book to go into a detailed analysis of the different messages contained in these utterances in terms of their social and inter-personal implications.[2] However, it must be accepted that they are phrased differently in order to convey different messages about the social relationship between the participants.

Any speech – be it natural or synthesized – carries these social overtones. Of course, it is debatable whether this is appropriate in the case of synthesized speech because the computer generating the speech cannot make conscious decisions about what social messages it should convey. Furthermore, there can be no personal relationship between a person and a machine and so judgements cannot be made about the relative positions in any hierarchy or other structure.

A machine will be programmed to make certain utterances. Canned speech might include words such as "please" and "thank you". In a sense this is an expression of the relationship between the programmer and the user of the system, but within an interaction it will be perceived by the user as a signal from the machine. Even though the user will be conscious that they are interacting with a machine, they will react to its politeness; they are more likely to be positively disposed to one that is (or appears to be) polite than one that is rude.

As the above examples suggest, to be polite often implies using more words. This may cause conflict. Some design principles for achieving rapid communication suggest that the number of words used be kept to a minimum, but the resultant utterance may sound curt and impolite.

---

[2] Interested readers will find more information in Walker et al. (1997), Nass and Moon (2000), Nass and Lee (2001) and Ribeiro (2002).

There are a number of factors that should be considered in attempting to set a level of politeness.

- *Stage of the dialogue*   In the early stages of a dialogue, when the relationship is being established, people tend to be more polite. The first utterance of a device might try to reflect this with an introduction such as "Welcome to…" Later utterances might drop these niceties.

- *User reactions*   People react to the level of politeness presented to them; if the device says "please" and "thank you" then the person will tend to use similar words in replying. That may or may not be desirable. In particular, in a speech input system it may be detrimental to evoke extra words that do not add to the surface meaning of the message but which may disrupt the speech recognition (Yankelovitch et al., 1995).

- *User competence*   An experienced user probably wants to get on with the task in hand and not be held back waiting for polite but unnecessary words.

- *Urgency*   If an utterance is urgent, such as a warning, then verbosity may be dangerous and terseness is not perceived as rude.

4.9 Presenting Numbers

Interactive systems are frequently required to give quantitative responses: distances, capacities, times, etc. By definition a number will nearly always be new information.

Many phrases consist of a number accompanied by supporting information that indicates how the number is to be interpreted. For example,

> 528416739 bytes free on disk

A simple speech synthesizer might read this as

> five two eight four one six seven three nine bytes free on disk

which is almost completely useless. The utterance is too long for the listener to remember and process into a meaningful form.

There is a way in which people speak numbers – one that has not evolved arbitrarily and should be applied when presenting numbers in a speech system. It is important to know the magnitude of a number quickly, so we read from left to right, starting with the most significant digit. We also insert magnitude indicators into the number: "thousand", "hundred", etc. It is not difficult to write software that will parse a number and pronounce it in this natural, human way. For example, if the number above were pronounced as

> five hundred and twenty eight million, four hundred and sixteen thousand, seven hundred and thirty nine

then primacy implies that the listener is likely to remember at least the first section and be aware that the number is something over 500 million. Thus, with suitable formatting, it should be possible to present most of the figures encountered in interactive systems with reasonable confidence that they will be recalled by the user.

However, before doing so one should also ask whether the whole of the number is relevant information. There is little point in taxing the user's memory with a number correct to nine significant digits if the user only requires the figure correct to two significant digits.

For example, requests for details of disk usage in many computer systems return figures in bytes. Thus if a user attempts to discover how much space remains free on a 10 GB hard disk the answer will be a number that may contain up to eleven digits. In practice it is unlikely that the user will need such precision. A user attempting to find out if there is enough space on the disk to accommodate a new piece of software, for example, is unlikely to have worked out the space required to the nearest byte. Thus a more appropriate response might be a number correct to two, or perhaps three, significant digits. If the user requires more precision this could be provided in response to further requests.[3]

If a number is new information then it follows that it should ideally be presented as the subject of a tone group, and that each self-contained number should be placed in a separate tone group. However, the structure of such tone groups needs to be considered carefully. If a number is small then there seems to be no reason why it cannot be placed anywhere

---

[3] One has to wonder why the designer of the software that generated the free space message above chose to give such precision. Even for visual presentation, it is likely that an answer of 500 MB would be more useful (as is implemented in the Macintosh MacOS system).

within a tone group, or at least, wherever is most appropriate in terms of the syntactic structure. If, on the other hand, a number is so long that it can be expected to occupy most of the listener's memory, then there are good arguments for placing it at the end of a tone group where it will be followed by a period of silence.

Deciding precisely whether a particular number can be regarded as small or large is more difficult, but the research findings discussed earlier provide some useful pointers. A number that consists of five or fewer digits can almost certainly be regarded as small. Even if considered as a string of unrelated digits it will not exceed the digit span of the average person, and if chunked appropriately it will occupy considerably less space in memory. Numbers with more than five digits may exceed a listener's short-term memory capacity if stored as individual digits, but the research suggests that if chunked suitably they can be stored and recalled without problems.

Before leaving the topic of numbers, we should consider special cases such as telephone numbers, credit-card numbers, dates, etc.

Telephone numbers and credit-card numbers present a particular problem because they are quite long, but must be presented in such a way that the listener can recall ALL the digits. Research (such as that by Ryan, 1969) has shown that recall of long numbers is improved if the number is broken down into smaller groups and pauses inserted between the groups. Wicklegren (1964) found that the highest rates of recall were achieved using groups of three digits each. Further research carried out by telecommunications companies has established that ten-digit telephone numbers are reliably recalled if presented as two groups of three digits and one group of four digits, all separated by pauses of around 1 second duration (Waterworth, 1983).

Dates are another special case. A human reader would probably render the number 1955 as "one thousand, nine hundred and fifty-five", but if it were a date they would be more likely to say "Nineteen fifty-five".[4] Context will often be sufficient to mark that a number is a date so that it may be spoken correctly.

---

[4] It is interesting that consensus has yet to be reached as to how we should read twenty-first century dates. Some people are comfortable with "two thousand and one" while others believe that "twenty oh one" is correct, presumably by consistency with previous centuries.

4.10 Summary

In view of the research findings reviewed in Chapter 2, it is proposed that designers should first consider the use of non-speech sound before turning to speech. Non-speech sounds can be used to convey many types of information and have the advantage that – if properly designed – they are less distracting and intrusive than speech.

Assuming the designer chooses to use the speech, the next issue is the design of the spoken message. An important part of this process is to identify the relative importance of each element of the message. This is based on the concept of new and given information, introduced in Chapter 2. Examining this topic in a little more depth reveals that there are many different categories of new and given information that the designer should be aware of.

Given information can be marked as being less important than new information through the appropriate use of prosody. However, in some cases it may be better to remove some or all of the given information in order to reduce the amount of information being communicated. It is noted that much spoken communication uses minor (i.e. non-grammatical) sentence forms, and that these are usually shorter than equivalent major sentence forms. However, if used appropriately they can convey the same information.

Further gains in efficiency can be achieved by avoiding sentence types that are not commonly found in speech, and which may be difficult to understand when heard rather than read. The research reviewed in this chapter suggests that there are considerable variations in memorability and response time, etc., between different kinds of sentence, and that passive and negative sentences in particular are probably best avoided.

Choosing the precise wording of a message is also important. Certain types of word take longer to recognize and respond to than others, and therefore should be used with care or if possible avoided altogether. Potentially problematic words include those that have multiple meanings, and those that are indistinguishable from other words when spoken. Problems may arise with some words because of limitations in the pronunciation rules used by speech-synthesizers. Designers should also take care to avoid ambiguity in the choice of words and phrases, since this may reduce the efficiency of spoken communication.

Numbers are in some ways a special case. They are almost invariably important, but if long may be difficult to recall. The designer should consider carefully just how much precision is actually needed, and present it with suitable indications of magnitude ("thousand", etc.). Where all the digits of a long number must be communicated, as in the case of telephone numbers, etc., digits should be spoken in small groups with pauses between them.

Further Reading

Halliday (1967a)
Chafe (1970)
Dahl (1976)
Prince (1981)
Brown (1983)

Presenting Individual Speech Dialogues

5

Having chosen the semantic structure of a dialogue, the final step is to choose the prosodic structure. This involves selecting an appropriate intonation pattern, then arranging the length of the words to fit a suitable rhythmic pattern.

5.1 Intonation Patterns in Spoken English

The intonation patterns used in spoken English vary enormously. If we were to record a selection of people speaking the same words, we would probably find that no two would use exactly the same intonation pattern. However, we would find certain marked similarities, and if we listened closely enough we might notice certain intonation patterns cropping up again and again. If we were to investigate further, we would find that intonation patterns are determined not only by sentence structure and type (question, statement, etc.) but also by factors such as the relationship between speaker and listener (deference, superiority, etc.).

Predicting the intonation pattern a speaker might use for a particular sentence in a given situation is very difficult. However, as Halliday pointed out, tone groups in natural speech generally exhibit one of a fairly limited number of intonation patterns (see Chapter 2). By adopting a few simple rules based on his analyzes, we should be able to choose intonation patterns that satisfy the basic requirements and sound right to the listener.

Halliday identified five basic intonation patterns used in the presentation of tone groups. He referred to these as the primary tones. They are illustrated in Figure 5.1. Each tone has characteristic intonation patterns for both the pretonic segment and the tonic segment. Figure 5.1 shows

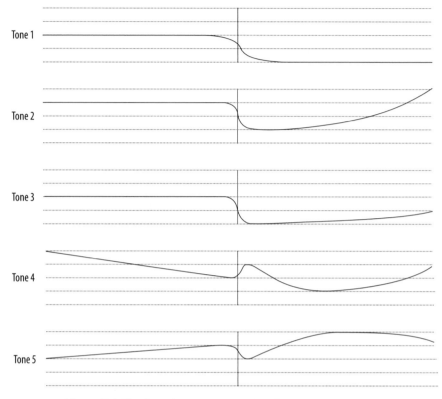

Figure 5.1 The five primary tones, as identified by Halliday.

both segments for each tone, but it should be borne in mind that tone groups will sometimes contain only the tonic segment.

Each of the tones displays a relatively sharp change of pitch at the beginning of the tonic segment. In Tone 1 this takes the form of a steady fall to a new pitch, in Tones 2 and 3 there is an abrupt drop to a lower pitch, and in Tones 4 and 5 there is a rapid fall-and-rise (or rise-and-fall) at this point. This is tonic prominence, the point at which the most important information in the tone group is placed. From this point onwards the pitch changes much less sharply throughout the remainder of the tonic segment.

The pretonic segment (where one is present) usually shows no pitch movement at all or gradual pitch movement in one direction (i.e. either rising or falling). It will be noted that in each case the pretonic shows less movement than the associated tonic. In Tones 1, 2 and 3 there is no pitch change in the pretonic and all the pitch movement is in the tonic.

In Tones 4 and 5 the pitch does change during the pretonic but far less dramatically than in the associated tonics.

According to Halliday, each of the five tones is associated with one or more basic language functions, such as statements, questions, directives and so on. However, it is not simply the case that there is one tone for statements, another for directives, and so on. There are certain tones that are used solely or largely for a particular function, such as issuing a statement or asking a question, but in general the difference between the five tones is not functional but semantic. Each tone carries a particular meaning, and when a statement or question is spoken with a particular tone, the meaning associated with that tone is added to the semantic information carried by the words themselves, as is illustrated in the following examples.

Tone 1 is generally neutral, meaning that it adds little if anything to the semantic content of the words themselves. It is the tone normally used for statements, for example,

- Peter sighed
- Helen lives in Leeds
- Michael put the box on the table

Tone 1 is the most commonly used of the five tones in spoken English.

Tone 1 is also used for "wh" questions, those beginning with words such as "who", "what" and "why". For example,

- Where are you going?
- Why didn't he answer?

"Wh" questions are the only questions in English that are sometimes spoken with a falling rather than a rising intonation pattern. Again, the tone is neutral, adding no further semantic information. The fact that the utterance is a question is clearly signalled as soon as the "wh" word is spoken, and therefore there is no further need to indicate that it is a question.

Tone 2 is also neutral in most cases and is the normal intonation pattern used for "yes/no" questions. These are questions that demand an affirmative or negative reply, for example,

- Will Michael resign?
- Are you satisfied?

As for all question types other than "wh" questions, this pattern shows a rise in pitch towards the end of the tone group.

Tone 2 is also sometimes used for "wh" questions, but in this case it is not semantically neutral. For "wh" questions, Tone 1 is neutral while Tone 2 makes the question tentative or deferential. For instance, the question "Where are you going?" spoken with a rising Tone 2 intonation, might imply that the speaker is puzzled that you are going away at all.

Tone 3 is generally the least forceful of the tones. Therefore it can be used to imply such qualities as dependence, politeness, deference, servility and incompleteness. It is also used to express reassurance. It is commonly used for statements, where it conveys either deference ("I'll do as you ask") or reassurance ("They'll soon be here"). It can also be applied to directives (which are sometimes known as commands), for example,

- Tell me all about it.
- Don't stay out too long.
- Give him a chance.

Tone 3 has the effect of making directives polite but otherwise neutral.

Tone 4 conveys an element of uncertainty or irresolution. It is normally used for statements, and adds the unspoken message "this may seem clear and simple, but in fact there is more here than meets the eye". It may also be used for directives, where it implies compromise or concession ("At least give him a chance").

Tone 5 is in many respects the converse of Tone 4. It conveys certainty and finality. It is normally used for statements, and adds the unspoken message "there may appear to be some doubt or uncertainty here, but in fact all is clear".

The use of intonation in this way allows speakers to convey information that would have to be stated explicitly were the information to be presented in written form. This makes it possible to use short, simple structures in many situations where longer, more complex structures would be required in written English.

The sentences shown below, for example, can take on any of the meanings listed opposite them depending on which intonation pattern is used. In some cases the change of meaning extends to a change of function, for example, from a question to a statement. If these sentences were presented in written form the additional meaning would have to be stated explicitly by adding further words.

Spoken sentence	Tone	Added meaning
Don't stay out too long	1	I mean it
Don't stay out too long	3	Not that you would
Give him a chance	1	That's an instruction
Give him a chance	4	Even though he'll probably fail
Peter isn't here yet	1	I notice
Peter isn't here yet	3	Is that so?
John	1	Stop it!
John	2	Is that you?
John	3	I've got something to say to you
(Examples taken from Halliday, 1970).		

In most cases the most appropriate intonation pattern will be the one that gives a neutral tone for the particular type of sentence being presented. These tones are:

- Statements   Tone 1
- Yes/no questions   Tone 2
- Alternative questions   Tone 2 (with each of the alternatives on Tone 1)
- "Wh" questions   Tone 1
- Directives   Tone 3

We will look at examples of each of these in turn.

5.2 Statements

As might be expected, the vast majority of the outputs produced by most interactive systems are statements. Of these, a small percentage are warning statements. Of the remaining outputs, most are questions and a small number are directives.

Statements are used to respond to requests for information, to indicate the progress of an operation, or to indicate which of several possible outcomes has occurred in practice.

Many of the statements found in interactive systems are already in minor sentence form, and could be presented as speech with few changes other than the addition of suitable prosody. We will take some statements from existing systems and use them as examples:

- Print queue is empty
- Traffic flowing freely
- Cooking complete

5.2.1 Intonation Patterns

We saw in Section 5.1 that each of the five tones includes a sharp change in pitch – known as pitch prominence – that coincides with the new information in the speech. Therefore, the first step in fitting an intonation curve to these statements is to identify the new information.

As we saw in Chapter 4, identifying the new information in speech is not always straightforward. However, in each of these cases, we can be reasonably confident that the new information is contained in the final word. If you're not certain as to why this should be, imagine an action that might produce each of these responses, phrase it as a request, then note what parts of the request also appear in the response. These are given information. The parts that don't appear in the question are the new information.

For example:

- *Request:*   Print queued documents
- *Response:*   Print queue is empty

If you think in these terms, it should be clear that the first part of each of these three statements merely reflects the question or, if you prefer, reminds the user what operation is being undertaken: checking the print queue, requesting traffic news, etc. Since the user may be presumed to have initiated the command, this will not be new information. It is the last word of each statement that carries new information – information about the outcome of the operation.

In applying an intonation curve to the above statements, therefore, pitch prominence would be given to the last word in each case.

However, where a word has more than one syllable, only one will be given pitch prominence. The syllable that receives pitch-prominence is the one that normally takes the stress when the word is spoken. The first two statements above both end with words that carry the stress on the first syllable, i.e.

<u>emp</u> - ty   <u>free</u> - ly

(if you're not sure why it should be the first syllable that is stressed, try speaking these words aloud with the stress on the second syllable, e.g. emp - <u>ty</u>, free - <u>ly</u>: you should find that these words sound very strange when spoken like this).

Therefore, the change in pitch which marks the new information in these statements should be placed not on the whole of the last word but just on the first syllable of the last word.

The third statement ends with a word that carries the stress on the final syllable, i.e.

com - <u>plete</u>

Therefore, the change in pitch that marks the new information in this statement should be placed on the final syllable of the last word.

Example intonation patterns for these statements are shown in Figure 5.2.

The examples above use Halliday's Tone 1, which is the neutral tone for statements. However, there may be occasions on which one of the other tones is appropriate. A possible example is the use of Tone 3 to give the statement an air of urgency appropriate to a warning. For example, "Entering a new program will over-write the old one." is a statement. However, replacing the existing program may be unintentional, so it is appropriate to add a suggestion of warning to the statement.

In the examples above, the general shape of the intonation curve is indicated but not the exact pitches to be used. In spoken English, patterns such as those shown may be uttered at almost any pitch within the speaker's vocal range. How does the designer of a speech-based system decide what the average frequency of an utterance should be, and by how much the pitch should rise and fall around the average?

Some of the rules governing pitch were examined in Chapter 2. It was noted that where a number of clauses follow one another within a breath group, the first clause is usually presented at a relatively high average pitch and each successive clause has a lower average pitch than

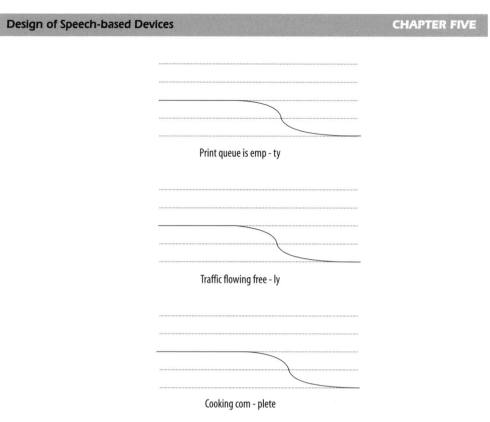

Figure 5.2 *Suggested intonation patterns for the example statements.*

its predecessor. In addition, the pitch-range declines with each successive clause, with the first clause showing a large rise and fall in pitch while later clauses show progressively smaller rises and falls.

Where a clause is presented on its own, there is much more variety in presentation. Freed from the need to place clauses within a structure, it seems, speakers choose the average pitch and degree of pitch variation of their clauses according to quite other criteria, perhaps including the desire to create dramatic and other effects.

It is difficult – and probably unnecessary – to define comprehensive rules for the presentation of single clauses. Given that suitable intonation is clearly of help to a listener, the best approach may be to make maximum use of the available range. In other words, set the average pitch of the speech somewhere in the middle of the available range and provide a wide degree of rise and fall around it. Provided the end result is not so extreme as to sound unnatural, it should be acceptable – and helpful – to the listener.

Indeed, there is some evidence that exaggerated intonation curves present no problems to listeners, and may even be helpful, provided the shape of the curve is correct. Research such as that conducted by Stevens et al. (1994b, 1995) suggests that placing exaggerated pitch-prominence on new information can help users find this information easily.[1]

5.2.2 Rhythm and Stress

Having considered the intonation pattern, the rhythmic structure also needs to be considered carefully. The basic principles are explained in Chapter 2. A passage of speech is broken up into a series of "feet", similar to musical bars. Each foot contains a number of syllables, the first of which is accented in some way (e.g. by being delivered at a slightly higher volume than the others). These accented syllables are known as salient syllables, while the non-accented syllables are known as weak syllables. Single-syllable content words are normally placed on salient syllables while single-syllable function words are normally placed on weak syllables. For multi-syllable words, the stressed syllable falls on a salient syllable regardless of where it occurs within the word.

---

[1] Stevens' work concerned the presentation of mathematical information to blind students using speech (Edwards, 1998a, 1998b). Mathematics relies to a large extent on visual notations, and without access to such notation, blind people are greatly hampered in any activity that uses mathematics. Non-visual alternative representations have to be used instead, and one candidate is speech. A problem with speech is that it can be ambiguous, whereas mathematics must be precise. For instance the two equations

$$3x + 4 = 7 \quad \text{and} \quad 3(x + 4) = 7$$

are mathematically different, but if they are read as "Three x plus four equals seven" either interpretation might be applied.

Stevens found that mathematicians can convey the differences between the two interpretations through speech by appropriate used of prosody. Using the same words, but changing the way they are spoken, the speaker can indicate the presence of the brackets in the second equation. In this instance, the bracketed sub-expression is signalled by a pause before it is spoken and a drop in pitch when speaking "x plus four".

Stevens developed a set of rules for the speaking of algebra, based on measurements of human speakers. Given the limitations of text-to-speech synthesis, he explored the effects of slightly exaggerating the parameters (pause length, pitch variation etc.) presented to the synthesizer. He found that this was in no way detrimental, and in most cases aided the listener in interpreting the speech.

In the first statement above, all the words except "is" are content words. Therefore, the salient syllables of these words will be stressed, and will occur at roughly regular intervals to form the rhythm.

In the first statement, "print" and "queue" are single-syllable words and, as we have already noted, "empty" is a two-syllable word that takes its stress on the first syllable. Therefore "print", "queue" and the first syllable of "empty" should each be placed on the first (strong) syllable of a foot. The function word "is" and the second syllable of "empty" should be placed on weak syllables. A suitable rhythm would be:

|| print | || queue | is || emp - | ty ||

In this example, "print", "queue" and the first syllable of "empty" occur at regular intervals. The first foot, containing the single-syllable word "print", must last as long as the following feet, even though these contain two syllables each. Therefore "print" is held for longer than the other syllables, or followed by a silent pause, in order to maintain the rhythm.

This is a valid rhythm, but you may feel it sounds a little slow and pedantic (try saying it aloud and see how it sounds to you). In practice, speakers might treat "print" and "queue" as a single word (or hyphenated phrase) and only place stress on the first word, "print". The resulting rhythm might look like this:

|| print | queue | is || emp - | ty | ||

This rhythm has three syllables in each foot rather than two, and doesn't require a silent pause in the middle to complete the rhythm (the only silent pause comes after the last syllable, where it has no effect). Because of this, most people will find it sounds less laboured than the previous example.

It might appear that this statement could be made even shorter by omitting the function word "is". However, this would not necessarily improve matters. Simply removing "is" would destroy the rhythm of the statement, and as we have seen, rhythm is an important factor underpinning the intelligibility of speech. If "is" were omitted, it would either have to be replaced with a pause, or the word "queue" would have to be lengthened in order to preserve the rhythm. For example:

|| print - | queue | || emp - | ty | ||

Even though function words appear relatively unimportant, they should not be removed without careful consideration. Function words reduce ambiguity and facilitate comprehension: removing them may reduce the length of an utterance and so make it easier to hold in memory, but it may also increase the amount of effort required to comprehend an utterance.[2]

In the second statement, the first and second words take their stress on the first syllable. The last word, as we have already noted, also takes its stress on the first syllable. A suitable rhythm would be:

|| traf - | fic || flow - | ing || free - | ly ||

In this example, the first syllable of each word falls on a strong beat of the rhythm, while the second syllable of each word follows it on a weak beat.

In the third statement, the first word takes its stress on the first syllable while the second word takes the stress on the second syllable. Therefore these two syllables will fall on successive strong beats, and the intermediate syllables will fall on weak beats. A suitable rhythm would be:

|| cook - | ing | com - || plete | | ||

5.3 Questions

Questions are used in interactive systems to request information (e.g. parameters), to determine which branch to take at intermediate points within an interactive operation, and to confirm the user's desire to proceed with operations that are potentially dangerous or irreversible.

Questions can be categorized into three main types: Yes/No questions, Alternate questions and "Wh" questions. We will look at each type in turn.

---

[2]This may be one of the reasons why "telegraphic speech" utilities are used so little. Telegraphic speech utilities remove function words, and were once a common feature of text-to-speech systems. Manufacturers claimed that they reduced the amount of time it took to speak a passage of text. However, telegraphic speech utilities never gained much popularity among regular users of synthetic speech systems, such as blind computer-users.

5.3.1 Yes/No Questions

Many of the Yes/No questions found in interactive systems are already in minor sentence form, and could be presented as speech with few changes other than the addition of suitable prosody. Others are in major sentence form and might benefit from being changed before being presented through speech.

We will take some Yes/No questions from existing systems and use them as examples:

> Compare more files?
> Proceed with format?
> Are you sure you want to delete this file?

Note that while the first two examples are clearly questions, they have an imperative structure – i.e. they are written in the same way as a command or directive, and are turned into questions only by the context and by the presence of the question-mark at the end. However, this is as valid a structure in speech as it is in written text.

The third question is rather long, and better suited to graphical interaction than speech-based interaction. If we were thinking of using a question like this in a speech-based system, we might ask ourselves whether all of it is necessary. For example, we might assume that the user will remember the action that gave rise to this response – presumably a command to delete a file – and therefore conclude that the latter part of the question is entirely given information. In this case we could simplify the question to:

> Are you sure?

If the user does require further information (e.g. a reminder of the file-name involved), this can be supplied in response to a separate request.

Note that this question is in full interrogative form, and this too is as valid a structure in speech as it is in written text.

There are several possible intonation forms for Yes/No questions, the most widely used being Tone 2, which is neutral in meaning.

In the case of the first two questions above, the new information is contained in the last word, so the point of pitch prominence in the intonation curve will coincide with the stressed syllables of these words. "Files" only has one syllable so the whole word is given pitch prominence.

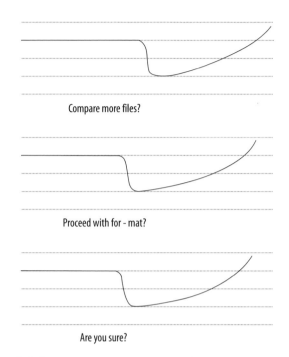

Compare more files?

Proceed with for - mat?

Are you sure?

Figure 5.3 *Suggested intonation patterns for the example questions.*

"Format" has two syllables with the stress placed on the first, so pitch prominence will coincide with the syllable "for".

If the third question is modified as suggested, the new information is also in the last word, "sure". Again, this is a single-syllable word, so the whole word is given pitch prominence.

The syllables that carry the new information will be placed on strong beats of the rhythm.

The first two questions have similar rhythmic structures because each begins with a word that takes its stress on the second syllable, i.e.

com - <u>pare</u>   pro - <u>ceed</u>

In the first example, a suitable rhythmic structure would place the second syllable of the first word and the only syllable of the last word on strong beats, for example:

| com - || <u>pare</u> | more || <u>files</u> | ...

In the second example, the last word has two syllables, of which the first takes the stress and should therefore be placed on a strong beat. A suitable rhythm would be:

| pro - | <u>ceed</u> | with || <u>for -</u> | mat

In practice, the two syllables of "format" might be rather more compressed than this suggests.

In the last example, all the words are one syllable long and the second word – "you" – is a function word. Therefore a suitable rhythm would place the "are" and "sure" on strong beats and "you" on a weak beat, for example:

|| <u>are</u> | you || <u>sure?</u> | ||

5.3.2 Alternative Questions

Another type of question commonly found in interactive systems is the alternative question, in which the questioner supplies a short list of alternatives from which the listener is invited to select. An example is the kind of response produced by many systems in the case of disk access failure, e.g.:

Retry, Cancel?

Note that this question is in minor sentence form. In its full, major sentence form it would be something like:

Do you wish to retry or cancel?

Alternative questions are normally spoken using Tone 2 for the stem of the question ("do you wish to…") and Tone 1 for each of the alternatives ("Retry", "Cancel"). Since only the alternatives are given here, each would be presented using Tone 1. Note that each word is new and therefore is given pitch-prominence within its own (brief) Tone 1 intonation pattern.

Both "retry" and "cancel" normally take the stress on the first syllable, so the rhythm would be:

|| <u>re -</u> | try | || <u>can -</u> | cel | ||

Note that the form used in many graphical systems is not a typical minor sentence form for an alternative question because it omits the "or" between the items. Therefore there is nothing other than context (and in the case of speech, phonology) to indicate that this is a question rather than a list-type statement. It could be made more obviously question-like by reinstating the "or", e.g.:

Retry or Cancel?

Adding the word "or" would not increase the time taken to present the question because the rhythm demands that the alternatives are presented at approximately regular intervals.

The added word should not disturb this rhythm, so it would replace the silent beat after the syllable "try", i.e.

|| <u>re -</u> | try | or || <u>can -</u> | cel | ||

thus making it clear that this is an alternative question without sacrificing brevity.

5.3.3 "Wh" Questions

Many "question" words in English begin with the letters "wh", for example, what, where, when, why, which and who. Questions built around these words are often referred to as "Wh" questions.

"Wh" questions are rarely used in interactive systems. This may be because "Wh" questions assume that a range of possible answers is recognized by both the questioner and the person to whom the question is put. For example, the question "which disk is the driver file on?" is only valid if the person responding knows how many disk-drives are attached to the system and how they are identified. If this knowledge cannot be assumed it will be necessary to list the disk-drives, in which case it would be more appropriate to use an alternative question (see above) or to invite the user to select a disk-drive from a menu or list.

If a "wh" question is used, it would normally be presented using Tone 1.

5.4 Directives

Most interactive systems contain very few directives. In most situations a question can be used in place of a directive, and this is often done in practice. For example, if we require information we can demand it, but we can also ask for it. In general, a system that makes requests will appear more "user-friendly" than one that makes demands.

Where directives are used, their function is normally to prompt the user to perform some operation, for example, to insert a disk or CD-ROM. Another common use is to instruct the user to press a key (e.g. "Hit any key to continue").

A typical directive might be phrased as follows:

> Insert Tools disk in drive A

This example is not well suited to speech presentation because it contains two items of information that appear to be new – the name of the disk, and the name (or letter) of the drive into which it should be placed. While it could be presented in this form, it would be better if it could be rephrased to form a simple directive containing just one item of new information.

It could be argued that the second item of apparently new information, the drive name or letter, is in fact given information. In most cases there will only be one disk with the given name and only one drive into which it will fit. For example, most computer systems only have one CD-ROM drive, so if the specified disk is a CD-ROM there is only one drive into which it can be inserted.

Thus in most cases the latter part of the phrase could either be presented as given information or discarded completely, e.g.:

> Insert Tools disk

In this form, the only new information is the single-syllable word "Tools", so this will receive pitch-prominence. A suitable intonation pattern would be Tone 3, which is neutral for directives.

The word "Insert" takes its stress on the second syllable, and "disk" only has one syllable. Therefore a suitable rhythm would be:

> | in - || <u>sert</u> | || <u>tools</u> | || <u>disk</u> | ||

The unstressed initial syllable should be much shorter than the three stressed syllables, which should occur at roughly regular intervals. This might be achieved by following each of the stressed syllables with a short, silent pause.

5.5 Summary

We have seen that intonation patterns in spoken English vary enormously, but that a wide range of meanings can be conveyed by applying a limited number of basic intonation patterns to different sentence structures (statement, directive, various types of question). Some examples were considered, illustrating the way in which changing the intonation pattern can alter the meaning of a sequence of words.

Following this, various sentence types were considered in turn, noting the relationship between sentence type, intonation pattern, and the location of new information within the sentence. The examples given should provide some guidance as to how designers might select the most appropriate intonation pattern for a particular task.

The issue of rhythm was also considered. As well as positioning syllables on strong or weak beats according to their status (stressed or unstressed syllable, function or content word), it was noted that some words may need to be increased or reduced in duration to fit the rhythmic pattern of the message. Alternatively, pauses may need to be added to complete the rhythm.

Further Reading

Halliday (1967a)
Chafe (1970)
Dahl (1976)
Prince (1981)
Brown (1983)

Presenting Lists and Menus

In Chapter 3 it was noted that there are certain responses produced by interactive systems that cannot easily be redesigned so as to produce an output that can be accommodated within a single speech tone group. In most cases this is because the output takes the form of a list.

Lists are widely used in interactive systems (for example, lists of files, menus of options, etc.), and the ability to scan a list, compare information on a number of items and subsequently make an informed choice is therefore an essential prerequisite for successful operation of such systems. While this task is comparatively simple using visual cues, it is vastly more difficult when the list is presented through speech.

6.1 Problems Posed by Spoken Lists

Pitt (1996) conducted a detailed study of the way in which a particular blind person used a speech-adapted computer. He noted that this individual encountered considerable difficulties when trying to use directory-listing commands. The subject made almost no use of such commands, preferring to use memory and trial-and-error approaches in locating files and navigating around the directory structure.

It is not difficult to find explanations for the apparent drawbacks of speech presentation when compared with visual presentation of lists. A person faced with a visually presented list can switch the focus of attention rapidly from one point to another and employ high-level reading skills such as looking for words of a particular length or with a particular pattern of ascenders and descenders. Such strategies allow people to identify likely targets within a list easily and quickly.

These strategies cannot be employed when the list is presented through speech. The user is forced to listen to each item in turn until the desired item is found. This imposes a more-or-less fixed minimum time for the search. Some improvement can be achieved by allowing the user to search the list interactively, moving up or down as desired and muting the speech of one item as soon as the cursor is moved onto another item. It was observed that this was how the subject of the study mentioned above chose to tackle the problem on those occasions when he did resort to a directory-listing command, and it appears that this method is commonly employed by users of screen-readers. However, even with this facility the user of a speech-based system is still placed at a considerable disadvantage compared with someone accessing a visually presented list.

The problem is even more acute when the task is not one of simple recognition but includes an element of recall. Tasks which involve searching a list for a group of related items, or looking for a particular item among a group (for example, the cheapest), require that the user compare information on several items simultaneously. This is comparatively simple when the list is presented visually: having identified the items for comparison the user can shift the focus of attention rapidly between them. Thus the screen or printed surface acts as a form of external memory and the amount of information which has to be stored in the user's own memory is kept to a minimum. When a similar task has to be performed with a spoken list, the user is forced to hold all the necessary information in memory. This increases the difficulty of the task and imposes much tighter constraints on the number of items that can be compared, hence considerably increasing the time required for such tasks.

6.2 Organizing Lists and Menus to Aid Memorization

It has long been recognized that organization aids memorization and learning, and that human beings strive to identify patterns and meaning in any information presented to them. The psychologist Bartlett recognized this when he coined the phrase "Effort after meaning" to describe the way in which subjects performing many different tasks seek to organize data in order to make it more memorable and easier to work with (Bartlett, 1932).

Other work has demonstrated clearly that this principle applies to spoken as well as written information.

A number of studies have shown that lists of associated words are easier to learn than lists of un-connected words (for example, Jenkins and

Russell, 1952) and that lists of apparently unconnected words become significantly easier to learn if the subject is supplied with a semantically meaningful linking attribute (Tulving and Pearlstone, 1966). It has also been shown that large quantities of data can be memorized more easily if presented in a hierarchical structure (Bower et al., 1969) or in some other organized way such as a matrix (Broadbent et al., 1978).

The question, then, is what sort of organization might prove useful? Pitt and Edwards (1997) conducted an experiment to find out how lists of filenames might be organized in order to make them more memorable when spoken rather than presented visually. In this experiment, subjects were asked to memorize sixteen different filenames and then recite them, from memory, into a microphone that was connected to recording equipment. When the recording was complete, subjects were asked what conscious decisions they had made regarding the ordering of the filenames and invited to comment on the process of memorizing and recalling the filenames. It was hoped that this would reveal what kinds of organization most facilitate the learning of lists of filenames.

Analysis of the recordings showed that:

- Subjects tried to organize all the filenames into groups. None of the subjects attempted to memorize the filenames as a single continuous list. Instead, all broke the filenames down into a number of smaller groups (usually four). While some of the filenames were obviously related to one another, others had no apparent relationship to any other filename. In spite of this subjects often grouped apparently unrelated filenames together. It appeared that it was much easier to remember the 16 filenames if they were grouped under a smaller number of headings.

- Filenames that could not be fitted into a group were presented last and were most likely to be forgotten. Some subjects were unable to find a meaningful way of grouping certain filenames. They invariably left these filenames until last. These filenames were more likely to be forgotten or recalled incorrectly than any of the grouped filenames.

- Subjects attempted to find mnemonic links between groups. Subjects generally recited the groups in order of size, starting with the largest group. It appeared that this most often represented what was for them the strongest link. However, some subjects reported that they had consciously ordered the groups so that there was a link from one group to the next. For example, one subject grouped together three

93

filenames that included the word "thesis" and placed the filename THESIS.OLD as the last of the three, using this as a mnemonic link to the filename MAIL.OLD which formed the first item of the next group.

These results suggest that it is difficult for people to hold long lists of items in memory, but that organizing them into smaller groups makes it much easier.

The results also suggest that quite simple forms of organization can be helpful in the memorization of filenames. Some of the linking attributes used by the subjects were highly subjective and could not easily be incorporated into a set of rules, but others were straightforward and could easily be implemented in software. For example, much of the organization observed in this study was simply based on matching strings of characters, such as grouping together all the filenames that included the word "thesis". This can easily be achieved in software.

6.3 List Size and Memorability

Organizing items into small groups may aid recall, but what is the maximum number of items that can be grouped together without any being forgotten?

There is no simple answer to this – it depends upon the type of items and what the subject knows of them.

In the study described above, the size of the groups used varied from subject to subject. The average size was between three and four, but in some cases subjects placed as many as five filenames in a single group. However, it was noted that the larger the group, the more likely it was that some items would be forgotten.

Miller (1956) reviewed the psychological research on memory published up to that time and came to the conclusion that people can recall between five and nine items at a time – seven plus-or-minus two. However, as pointed out in Chapter 3, this does not necessarily mean five-to-nine words or digits. The emphasis is on "items", and an item may be one word (or number, or whatever) or many.

Many psychological studies have examined serial recall for spoken material, including recall of word lists. Most of these studies have used either standard English words or nonsense words. The findings from some of these studies could probably be applied with little difficulty to spoken menus since most menu items are standard English words or short phrases comprising standard English words (for example, Open, Save, Cut, Paste, etc.).

However, some types of information found in interactive systems pose more significant problems. Names are one example. Unlike words found in a dictionary, names may be entirely novel and therefore more difficult to recall. Even familiar names may be hard to recall if used in unfamiliar combinations. For example, if we hear a list of people's names read out, we will probably find most of the individual Christian and surnames familiar and have no difficulty recalling them in isolation. However, recalling a list of familiar Christian and surnames in unfamiliar combinations may prove more difficult.

A similar problem arises with place names. Many place names contain familiar elements – for example, "town", "bridge", "ford", "castle", etc. – but this does not necessarily make it easy to recall new place names. Even when familiar elements are present, they may appear in unexpected positions and/or be interspersed with unfamiliar elements. Remembering an unfamiliar ordering of familiar elements is not necessarily any easier than recalling a completely novel string.

Computer file names present an even more difficult problem. They may be chosen at the whim of the user and often contain acronyms, abbreviations or a series of concatenated words. They may also contain several elements separated by full stops or other punctuation characters. Such names may prove very difficult to remember when spoken.

Pitt and Edwards (1997) conducted a further study in order to determine peoples' ability to recall spoken lists of filenames. A list of 48 DOS-style filenames (i.e. filenames with three-character extensions, such as "foo.txt" and "bar.doc") were loaded into a computer program which reproduced them in random order through a speech-synthesizer. The filenames could be spoken in groups of either two, three or four, with the program waiting after each group until a key was pressed before speaking the next group. Three groups of subjects took part. They were asked to listen to the speech, and then to write down what they had heard before pressing the key to hear the next group of filenames. All three groups of subjects heard the same 48 filenames, but one group heard them spoken in pairs, one group heard them spoken in threes and one group heard them spoken in fours.

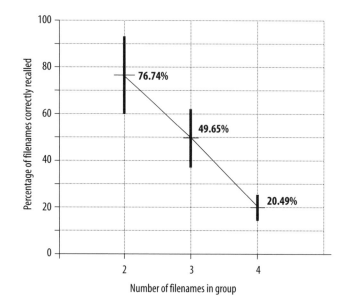

Figure 6.1 Graph showing the percentage of DOS-style filenames correctly recalled when presented through synthetic speech in groups of two, three or four. The black bars show the standard deviation from the average score.

The results of this experiment are shown in Figure 6.1. It can be seen that even when the subjects heard only two filenames at a time they recalled on average only 76.74% of them correctly. When the filenames were presented in groups of three the recall rate dropped to below 50% and when the filenames were presented in groups of four the recall rate was only just over 20%.

These results indicate the problems faced by those attempting to communicate lists of items through speech. While standard English words can probably be communicated with reasonable reliability in groups of five to six or more, some types of information – such as filenames – cannot reliably be communicated even in much smaller groups.

However, the situation is not so bad if filenames are presented in groups of related items rather than randomly chosen items. Following on from the study described in Section 6.2, Pitt and Edwards (1997) conducted a study in which filenames were sorted and those with shared elements grouped together. The filenames were then spoken in groups, with the user choosing when a new group should be spoken. Within the groups, prosody was used to highlight the similarities and differences between

Table 6.1 *Percentage of filenames recalled when presented either in randomly selected groups or in sorted groups (all filenames share a common element)*

	Number of filenames in each group					
	2	3	4	5	6	7
Randomly selected filenames	76.7%	49.7%	20.5%			
Related filenames		89.1%	77.1%	71.2%	66.7%	56.25%

the individual filenames. For example, three filenames that contained the string "thesis" were grouped together; the string "thesis" was presented at the same pitch each time it occurred, while the other, dissimilar elements of the three filenames were presented as new information and given pitch-prominence (see Section 6.5). Under these circumstances, the rate of recall improved dramatically. A comparison between the results obtained in this study and the results obtained in the study described earlier is shown in Table 6.1.

6.4 A Speech-based, List-searching Tool

A speech-based tool that presents lists as a series of groups is described in Pitt and Edwards (1997), Pitt (1998). The tool was designed to help blind people explore the contents of computer directories using speech, but many of the principles it employs could be applied to other tasks that involve exploring lists and menus using speech.

In order to ease the task of examining the files within a directory, the tool uses an algorithm that sorts the filenames by grouping together those with shared strings of characters. This algorithm is based on the results of the studies described in Section 6.2 and 6.3, and incorporates a variety of rules to enable it to identify valid groupings and reject invalid ones.[1]

---

[1] The algorithm identifies matching strings, then ranks the matches primarily in order of length. However, it also incorporates rules to identify strings that match but may not indicate related filenames. It does this principally by ignoring apparent matches that rely on function words and common sequences of letters, for example "the" and "ing", unless they are part of a longer matching string. For example, the algorithm would group together the filenames "Lit Review" and "Lit Survey" because they both contain the three-letter string "lit", but would not group together the filenames "Lathe Manual" and "Leather Design" even though both contain the four-letter string "athe".

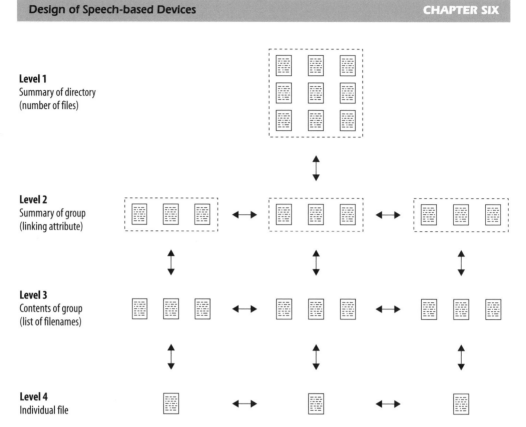

Figure 6.2 Diagram illustrating the operation of the list-searching tool. At the top level, the directory is identified. At the second level, a group is identified. At the third level, the individual filenames within a group are identified, and at the fourth level an individual file is selected.

Once the items in the list have been sorted into groups, the user can explore the list interactively, moving up and down a hierarchical structure to hear either an overall summary, a list of the groups, the contents of one of the groups, or details of an individual file.

The operation of the tool is illustrated in Figure 6.2. When it is started up, the user is told how many files the directory contains. On moving down to the second level (by pressing the DOWN cursor key), the user is told how many groups the directory has been sorted into and what those groups are called. The group names are based on the linking attributes identified by the sorting algorithm. This is usually the longest string of characters common to all the files in that group. For example, the three filenames mentioned earlier, all of which include the string "thesis", would be placed in a grouped named "thesis".

If the directory is very large and has been sorted into a correspondingly large number of groups, the list is not read-out in full but divided into shorter lists. Repeated movements in one direction will take the user back to the start of the list. Prosody is used to signal the start and end of the list, and to give the listener an approximate idea of the length of the list and the position of the current item within it (see Section 6.5).

Pressing the DOWN cursor key while at the second level takes the user to the third level. Whichever group-name is being spoken (or has most recently been spoken) at the second level becomes the current group, and the names of the individual filenames in that group are spoken out. Again, if the list is long, it is divided into smaller sections which can be reached using the LEFT and RIGHT cursor keys, and prosody is used to help the listener identify the position of the current item within the list.

Moving down to the bottom level, the user is presented with a single file-name, that of the file whose name was last spoken at the third level. Moving left or right selects other files in the same group. Using single-key commands, the file can be examined further (e.g. to determine its size or date of last modification) or selected for use in an operation such as copying, moving or deleting.

Baddeley (1993) notes that performing any action while memorizing list items tends to enhance recall. He suggests that this is because the association between the action and the response produces a richer memory trace that is easier to recover. Therefore, in addition to any benefit gained by organizing the files into small groups, we might expect that making items available in response to keyboard actions would make them more memorable than the same items heard as a continuous list without intervention from the user.

6.5 Using Prosody to Convey Structure and Context

Organizing lists into small groups of related items is one way of aiding memorization, but using appropriate prosody may also help. Studies suggest that human beings use prosody to highlight links between items, pointing out structures that may not be apparent and underlining those that are.

This effect is commonly observed in the recitation of football results on the radio on a Saturday evening. Announcers use a conventional pattern that allows the listener to predict which team was the winner before the whole result has been announced. The score of the winning team is emphasized and spoken at a higher pitch, so that falling intonation across a result signals a home win, rising pitch indicates an away win and a flat presentation means a draw.

Pitt (1996) conducted a study of this phenomenon, in which subjects were asked to read lists of DOS-style filenames aloud as if to a blind person who needed to learn the lists. In this study the lists were written down in a fixed order, so subjects did not sort them into a preferred order as they did in the study described in Section 6.2. Instead it was noted that they appeared to be using prosody to indicate links between items in the list, even when those items were not adjacent to one another in the list.

Analysis of the responses suggests that, although the subjects all read the lists in the given order, they were mentally organizing the filenames into groups and were using prosodic cues (rhythm, pitch, loudness) to try to convey this organization to a listener.

As an example of the type of organization observed in the recordings, consider the sequence

   PROGRAM.C,   TEST.BAT,   NEWKEY.C

The intonation pattern used by one of the subjects when speaking this sequence is shown in Figure 6.3.

It can be seen that the first and third filenames (both of which include the phrase "dot c") are presented at a higher average pitch than the second filename. There is also a marked similarity between the intonation pattern used for the first and third filenames, and a sharp contrast between this pattern and that used for the second filename. The first and third

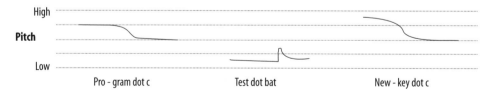

Figure 6.3 Example of the intonational structures used by subjects to convey relationships between filenames.

filenames have an intonation pattern that is marked by an initial period at a relatively high pitch followed by a smooth fall to a lower pitch. The starting pitch varies between the two, with the third filename beginning at a higher pitch than the first filename, but the final two syllables are delivered at the same pitch in both cases. By contrast, the second filename starts at a low pitch and finishes at a higher pitch, with a sharp rise followed by a more gentle fall in the middle. The complete sequence is preceded and followed by pauses (not illustrated in Figure 6.3) which are over twice as long as the pauses which separate the three filenames.

The effect of all this to strongly associate PROGRAM.C and NEWKEY.C in the mind of the listener, and to indicate that TEST.BAT is not related to the other two items. Furthermore, the fact that "program" and "newkey" are delivered at different pitches while "dot c" is presented at the same pitch each time it appears emphasizes the fact that the extension is common to both filenames while the section before the extension is different.

Prosodic structuring may also be observed even when the items in a list have already been organized into a suitable order. Analysis of the study described in Section 6.2 showed that prosodic structuring was clearly apparent in the subjects' recital of the lists. Every subject placed significantly longer pauses between successive groups of filenames than between the filenames within a group. The pauses placed between groups were almost invariably at least twice as long as those within groups and in some cases were five times as long or even more (although some of the longer pauses may have resulted from difficulties in recall rather than being intentional prosodic effects).

All of the subjects used intonation to emphasize the grouping of the filenames. The degree of variation in pitch varied considerably from subject to subject, as did the precise pattern of intonation used, but all showed at least the basic features of a rise in pitch at the start of each group and a fall in pitch at the end. Within groups, subjects appeared to be using pitch in much the same way as the subjects in the previous study (as illustrated in Figure 6.3). Those parts of filenames that were common to a group were generally presented at a lower pitch than those parts that differed. For example, when reciting the names of program files with ".c" extensions, all the subjects intoned the repeated phrase "dot C" at a lower pitch than the remainder of the filenames.

This high degree of consistency in the prosodic structures used by the subjects suggests that prosody is important. The subjects' use of pitch to indicate which part or parts of a filename differ from preceding ones corresponds with the research findings discussed in Chapter 2, in which it was seen that intonation is used to indicate the position of new information. The stress (indicated by pitch prominence) is placed on those parts of a filename that differ from previous filenames, while those parts that are the same are not stressed.

However, there are also differences between the prosodic patterns noted in this study and those discussed in Chapter 4. The main difference is that the subjects in this study treated each group of items as if it were a single tone group (identified by an initial rise in pitch, a final fall in pitch, and by the use of grammatical pauses to separate it from adjacent tone groups) but gave pitch prominence to several items in each group rather than to one.

This pattern does not precisely match any of the intonation patterns identified by Halliday, but it does have strong similarities with a number of the prosodic structures he describes. In particular, it bears a strong similarity to the pattern he observed being used for alternative questions, in which the speaker lists a number of alternatives and requires the listener to specify one of them when replying. For example:

    Shall we go to the cinema, the pub, or stay in and watch TV?

Halliday noted that the body of an alternative question is treated as one tone group while each of the alternatives – "cinema", "pub" and "watch TV" in this example – is given its own separate intonation pattern, complete with pitch prominence to mark the new information it contains (Halliday, 1970).

As might be expected, the pitch contour associated with alternative questions displays a typical questioning structure, with a sharp fall on the stressed syllable followed by a rise. This is quite different from the pattern observed in this experiment, in which the pitch remained low for given information (the repeated phrase "dot exe", for example) but rose when new information was presented. Of more interest is the pattern Halliday identifies for use with statements, commands and certain other types of questions. This pattern bears a striking resemblance to the prosodic patterns encountered in this experiment. The pitch falls as it approaches the new information and then rises gently on the first syllable of the new information.

Halliday gives an example of such a statement in which there is a list containing a repeated word. The example (Figure 6.4) he gives is

    I've read chapter one, chapter three and chapter four.

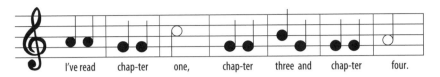

Figure 6.4 *Example of the use of rhythm and intonation in a statement that includes a list.*

In this case, the greatest stress falls on the final "four", but the rhythmic and intonational structure is such that the words "one", "three" and "four" are all stressed to some extent. Each is marked by a rise in pitch and each falls on the first syllable of a foot. Since each foot occupies approximately the same amount of time (see Section 2.1), the three words that represent new information are presented at regular intervals. It is not too difficult to see how it might help the listener to have the new information clearly signposted in this way.

In the light of the results obtained from the experiment and the previous research findings described above, it appears that organizing a list of names into suitably defined groups and using prosodic cues to highlight this organization is likely to aid the listener as well as the speaker. Therefore, it seems likely that we could make spoken lists of names easier to use by organizing them into meaningful groups and by reflecting this organization in the prosodic structure of the speech.

Prosody is used extensively in the list-reading tool described in Section 6.4. At the second level, where group names are spoken, prosody is used to indicate the length of the list and the location of the present item within it. The intonation rises at the start of the list and falls gradually as the list is read out, dropping sharply on the last item. If a file directory is very large and has been sorted into a correspondingly large number of groups, the list is not read out in full but divided into shorter lists. In this case, the prosody of the synthetic speech indicates that there are more group names to be heard, and the user can hear them by pressing the LEFT or RIGHT cursor keys. Repeated movements in one direction will cause the user to "wrap-around" back to the start of the list, whereupon the prosody of the speech makes it clear that the full list has been heard and that the user is now hearing parts of the list again. The same occurs if the user moves down to the next level and listens to individual filenames. Again, if the list is long, it is divided into smaller sections which can be reached using the LEFT and RIGHT cursor keys, and prosody is used to indicate the limits of the list.

As well as being used to indicate the start and end of spoken lists, prosody is used to help listeners grasp the relationships between files within a group. The interactive list-reading tool identifies repeated syllables and similar features within lists and uses prosodic-variation to highlight them. The nature and extent of the variations sounds somewhat coarse and exaggerated compared with natural prosody, but tests have shown that listeners still found the prosodic cues helpful.

Through the use of prosody and by allowing interactive exploration of a hierarchical structure, the interactive list-reading tool greatly eases the task of recovering information from long lists using speech. When evaluated in comparison with a conventional list-reading utility (which allows only sequential, linear exploration), it was found that subjects performed a practical task more than twice as quickly using this tool and also reported lower levels of effort and fatigue.

6.6 Using Priming Information

Research suggests that many types of information, whether visually or aurally presented, are easier to recall and interpret if the subject is first given a suitable context (for example, Bransford and Johnson, 1972). This is known as "priming".

Priming can be particularly useful when presenting large amounts of information through speech. It can reduce the amount of information a listener has to store in memory at a given time, and/or reduce the amount of mental effort required to interpret the information.

For example, consider the situation in which a blind person is playing the game Hangman, using a computer with speech output. The sequence of letters and spaces has to be held in memory as the unknown word is assembled, making the task much more difficult than it would be for a sighted person who can jot down the sequence of letters and spaces on paper.

At a certain stage in the game, the player may be told that the current sequence is "blank, A, blank, blank". Each time the player successfully guesses a letter, he or she will hear the sequence of letters and spaces spoken again, with the newly guessed letter added in the appropriate position(s). ("Blank, A, W, blank".) Listening to the new sequence of letters and spaces, the player will probably try to do several things simultaneously:

- The player will probably have one or more words – or at least parts of words – in mind as possible solutions, and will have guessed the most recent letter in an effort to check these possibilities. Therefore he or she will be testing the sequence against one or more expected sequences.

● Regardless of whether or not these expectations are met, the player will be trying to memorize the sequence.

Attempting to do the two things at once – memorize the sequence while also thinking about what it contains – is surprisingly difficult. A solution might be to try to memorize the sequence first and then think about its contents, but this also appears to be more easily said than done. In practice the listener often comes away with only part of the information, perhaps having determined that the previous guesses were wrong but not having worked-out exactly where the new letter fits into the sequence.

The problem can be eased by priming the listener, i.e. giving them some contextual information before the detailed information. In the case of a Hangman game, this could be done by stating whether the guessed letter appears in the word or not, and if it does, how many times it appears. This allows the listener to reformulate expectations and per-haps reject some possible solutions BEFORE listening to the sequence of letters and spaces.

Pitt and Edwards (1996) conducted a study involving a group of blind people playing a computer-game based on Hangman. The game was designed for use with a conventional visual display but had been adapted with the aid of a speech synthesizer. The aim of the study was to find out what sort of problems might arise when a program intended for visual display was adapted in this way.

A feature of the game was that it displayed the following line of text after each attempt at guessing a letter:

There are x occurrences of the letter y in the word

This was then followed by the sequence of letters and spaces comprising the word. Both were converted into speech by the speech-synthesizer.

It had been anticipated that the phrase before the sequence of letters and spaces would prove distracting. It appeared to be redundant since the listener could obtain the same information in more detailed form by listening to the sequence of letters and spaces. Moreover, it appeared to be excessively long. However, in practice the blind people playing the

105

game seemed to find it useful. It was observed that they rarely tried to mute it, and when asked about it afterwards most said that listening to it had helped prepare them for what followed.

This is a typical example of the way priming works. In this case it was entirely accidental, but the idea could be applied deliberately in many applications. For example, if we were designing a version of the Hangman game specifically for use with speech we might even extend the degree of priming provided. We could, for example, announce not only the number of occurrences of the guessed letter in the word, but also roughly where they occur. This would allow the listener to check his or her suspicions before starting to listen to the sequence of letters and spaces, fully primed to extract the maximum amount of information from listening to it.

6.7 Providing Summaries and Overviews

One of the powerful functions of sight is that one can take different views of the same scene. In particular, it is possible to take a glance at a scene to gain a quick overview of the information it comprises. The essence of the glance is that it is fast, and that this brevity is obtained at the expense of detail. The viewer can then decide how to proceed with whatever task they have. They may decide, for instance to focus on a particular part of the scene in order to obtain more detailed information from it.

Hearing does not generally have this facility. There are a number of reasons for this. One is related to the transitory nature of sounds. A sound exists in time and once it has passed it cannot be re-examined (at least not directly, although an internal representation of it may be replayed in the head, as discussed in Chapter 2). Also sound does not necessarily have a structure that lends itself to rapid analysis.

It is possible to use non-speech sounds to generate an auditory glance. The Maths Project tackled the problem of presenting mathematical formulas to blind people in an auditory form (Stevens et al., 1994a, 1996a, 1996b). One representation used was the earcon. Earcons were first suggested by Blattner et al. (1989) as symbolic, structured sounds. Within the Maths Workstation, sounds were structured to reflect the structure of the mathematics they represented, so giving the overview of a glance. Because earcons are symbolic, they have to be learned; the mapping from the sound to its meaning is often not intuitive. However, experiments have shown that some level of comprehension is rapidly learned. Such representations can be used in applications in which the users will be motivated to learn the meanings, or when the information embodied is largely redundant, so that it supports and enhances the interaction, but to miss it is not critical.

However, there are some sound mappings that are quite instinctive. For instance, in the Maths Workstation the beginning of an expression is marked by a sequence of notes rising in pitch, while the end is signalled by a falling sequence. This kind of sound can thus be used, for instance, to prime the listener as to the nature of the spoken information that is about to be presented. Utterances might be divided into categories, such as statements, warnings, questions and so on and then each could be preceded by a non-speech cue.

A particular example of the application of this idea is in aircraft warning systems. Patterson (1982) devised a scheme whereby when an error situation arises (or is about to arise) on an aircraft flightdeck a sound will be generated, giving information about the type and the urgency of the problem. This will usually be followed by a spoken message, so that the identity of the error is unambiguous.

Overviews and summaries can also be provided in a speech form. The list-searching tool described in Section 6.4 provides a form of glance by sorting filenames into groups and allowing the user to hear a list of the group names. Recent work has examined the possibility of doing something similar for the world-wide web. The web comprises a vast amount of information, to the extent that there is a fear of information overload. One mechanism that sighted people use to deal with this overload is the glance. We arrive at a new page and quickly scan it. Very often, this quick glance will tell us whether we are likely to find the information we require on the page, and we can then decide whether to move on to another page or invest time reading this one.

A blind web user, accessing the web through a speech-based interface does not have this facility. The browser is likely to attempt to read the page from top left to bottom right, at quite a slow rate, not picking out the items of interest. To overcome this problem, speech-based browsers such as BrookesTalk (Zajicek et al., 1998) attempt to simulate the glance by automatically summarizing the page contents. The content of the page is analyzed and a summary automatically generated. The summary is brief and so can be presented quite quickly in speech, thus playing the role of a glance.

6.8 Summary

We have seen that lists and menus, although simple to use when presented visually, pose considerable problems when presented through speech. Searching a list for a particular item is slow because the listener has little option but to work through the list sequentially, hearing each item in turn. Tasks that involve making comparisons or performing other operations on items in a list are even more difficult. What is required is some way of making lists easier to memorize and scan, thus simulating the facilities that make visual searching of lists so easy.

Memorability can be improved by organizing lists into small groups of related items. Numerous studies have shown that information becomes easier to remember when it is organized, provided it is organized in a way that is meaningful to the user. In some cases (such as menus), the items in a list may be more-or-less constant and the designer can choose an appropriate grouping. In other cases the list contents may be fluid (as in the case of filenames in a directory), in which case the user may not be able to select groupings. However, it may still be possible to design software that groups items using a set of rules.

Even when items are grouped in some meaningful way, the size of the groups will still affect memorability. If the group is too large, its contents will be difficult to recall. The research reviewed in this chapter suggests that groups of three, four or even five items can be recalled with relatively high levels of accuracy, provided the items within the group are related. However, when the items are not related, recall is poor even for very small groups.

Appropriate use of prosody can make recall easier. Prosody can be used to highlight the relationship between items in a group, indicating which parts of names, etc., are shared and which parts are unique. Prosody can also be used to provide contextual information, indicating roughly how long the list is and where the present item is located within the list. This information is readily available when lists are scanned visually, and it seems likely that providing the same kind of information to the user of a spoken list may aid searching and recall.

Memorability may be further improved by priming the listener, e.g. indicating what has changed in a list since last hearing before presenting the list again. Priming typically involves providing a short summary, and is particularly useful when a task involves relatively large amounts of information that may change often, as was the case in the "Hangman" game discussed in Section 6.6. It may be useful in many other situations, for example, when listing the contents of a "basket" of purchases in an on-line shopping system.

Finally, it was noted that summaries and overviews are useful in many other cases. They can provide the listener with some of the flexibility available when handling visually presented information through the use of glances. Many of the topics examined in this chapter are concerned with the provision of overviews of one kind or another, for example, grouping a set of files so that they can be identified by a common name, or summarizing the result of a guess in the "Hangman" game. The same principle can be applied in many other situations, providing the user of spoken information with at least some of the facilities readily available to users of visually presented information.

Case Studies

7.1 Introduction

This chapter brings together the theoretical material of the previous chapters and considers its practical application to speech-based devices. Two existing speech-based devices – a road traffic information device and a voicemail system – are reviewed, after which a design for a talking video recorder programmer is proposed.

7.2 Evaluation of the Trafficmaster Freeway

The Trafficmaster Freeway[1] is a road traffic information system that gives car drivers advance information regarding traffic flow to aid in avoiding delays. The system is based on sensors that are sited at intervals on major roads throughout the UK, monitoring the speed of the traffic. If the speed drops below a 30 mph average for a period of three minutes or more, the sensor sends an alert to a data centre. Information is broadcast out from that centre to transmitters. Each transmitter selects the information relating to its location and broadcasts it, to be picked up by receivers such as the Freeway in nearby vehicles. The Freeway can then communicate that information to the driver in the form of speech.

The Freeway is approximately $12 \times 9 \times 3$ cm or $4.75 \times 3.5 \times 1.25$ inch (see Figure 7.1). It can be mounted on the dashboard of the car in such a

---

[1] Trafficmaster PLC, University Way, Cranfield, Bedfordshire, UK, MK43 0TR.

Figure 7.1 The Trafficmaster Freeway.

position as to receive the broadcast signals. It has a very simple user interface consisting of a single pushbutton, a volume control wheel and an LED light – in addition to speech and some non-speech sound output. The speech is a digitized female voice of medium quality.

This is a good example of the appropriate use of speech technology. Driving is a visually demanding and safety-critical task. An auditory source of information will cause minimal disruption to the driving task, but the information to be imparted (which will be quite detailed for much of the time) requires the richness of speech.

7.2.1 Operation

The direction of travel of the vehicle can only be determined once the device has passed at least two transmitters. When the device first detects a signal the identity (and hence location) of the transmitter is noted. When a new signal is picked up, the position of the second transmitter relative to the first gives the direction of travel. This means that the first spoken message from the Freeway is rather unspecific: as much information as is available on all roads in the vicinity is given. For example, near a road junction, the first message might be:

(1) M1 southbound: traffic flowing freely. M1 northbound: slow moving traffic. Expect 5 minutes' delay. M62 eastbound: stationary traffic: avoid. M62 westbound: traffic flowing freely.

Once the course of the vehicle has been determined, more selective information is presented. For example, having entered the M1 southbound, the next message might be:

(2) You are near M1, junction 41 southbound. Traffic flowing freely.

Alternatively, if the driver is less fortunate, the message might be:

(3) You are near M1, junction 41 southbound. M1 southbound, very slow traffic for 4 miles. Between junctions 41 and 42 expect 10 minutes' delay.

The Freeway operates in two modes, automatic and manual. In automatic mode the Freeway will announce information only when it is new. For example, if information is received warning of a previously unannounced delay, a suitable message will be spoken automatically. On passing subsequent transmitters the message will be spoken spontaneously only if the information has changed (e.g. the delay has become longer or, alternatively, the road is now clear). If the information is unchanged, the device will beep and flash a green light as an indication that a transmission has been received but since it contains no novel information it will only be heard if the driver chooses to hear it (by pressing the button). Under good road conditions, the message at every transmitter will be "Traffic flowing freely" and the driver does not need to hear this; a beep and a flash are sufficient to confirm this to the driver.

In manual mode messages are not spoken automatically. The availability of any message is signalled with a flash of the light. A green light signals a clear road while a red light indicates a warning of a delay. The corresponding message will only be spoken if the driver presses the button.

7.2.2 Requirements

Under most circumstances, the Freeway should provide the driver with warnings of traffic congestion on his or her route well in advance. The information should be as full as possible – bearing in mind what is novel and what is known to the driver. It should be provided in a manner that does not cause annoyance. Speech, as pointed out earlier, is the ideal mode of delivery for most of that information. At the same time it is competing with other sources of auditory information in a rich audio space. As has been pointed out by Bill Buxton (1989) a driver operates in a rich auditory environment. He or she will be monitoring the note of the engine (as a cue indicating when to change gear), aware of external sounds such as sirens, may have the radio on and may be engaged in a conversation with a passenger. There is now an additional possibility – which was not the case when Buxton wrote his article – that the driver might also be engaged in a conversation on a telephone – though this is not to be recommended (Edwards, 1998a; Redelmeier and Tibshirani, 1997). The Freeway must thus compete with these other auditory messages. It must alert the driver to the arrival of information and then present it in such a way that it is audible and comprehensible but not excessively intrusive.

7.2.3 Analysis

All the information in example (1) above can be classified as novel, since the device has only just become active. It is quite a lot of information at one time. Nevertheless it may well be appropriate in the circumstances. The driver might equally well be planning to continue along any one of those four routes, and now has the all the information necessary to decide whether to continue with the original plan or modify it. Each of the potential routes is prefixed by its identity ("M1 southbound", etc.) which will help cue the listener for the pertinent information.

The speech is constructed from digitized fragments, and it is possible to "hear the joins" between them. Despite this, the quality of the speech is quite high. Good quality reproduction is appropriate in this application in which the speech will always be competing in a noisy environment. Good prosodic quality is achieved as well. With regard to timing, pauses are inserted between phrases to mark out the structure well (this is indicated in the transcriptions above by punctuation; a full stop for a long pause, a comma for a shorter one and so on). Similarly, intonation is used effectively. The utterances are essentially structured on sentences, and each sentence is spoken with an appropriate intonation.

Numbers under 100 are spoken as wholes, (e.g. "M twenty-five" not "M two-five") as is natural and would be expected in normal conversation. Higher numbers are spelled out (e.g. "A one zero three nine") but again that is what would be expected in most conversations (not the "A one thousand and thirty nine").

Once the direction of travel has been determined, the form of the messages changes, as in example (2) above. It is interesting that they become less abrupt in that they are prefixed with the phrase "You are near…". This does not add any useful information, but it might be argued that it acts as a cue, warning the user that pertinent speech is about to be delivered.

Once the driver is established on a route the messages can become tedious since they re-present known, old information, particularly the name of the road and direction of travel. If the Freeway has any memory, it should not be difficult to implement a very simple model of novel versus known information. This is discussed further below, in Section 7.2.5.

7.2.4 Non-speech Sounds

The Freeway does not make very extensive use of non-speech sounds. A single sound is used to convey the information that a spoken message is available, but that it does not contain any novel information. This is good use of a non-speech signal. The aesthetics of non-speech sounds are difficult to characterize, an extension of the generally difficult topic of which sounds cause annoyance. About all that can be safely said about auditory annoyance is that it is subjective; what one person finds acceptable may cause annoyance to another.

It is probable that some people will be annoyed by the beep that the Freeway makes. This sound will be heard frequently when driving on the average motorway, so in choosing the sound it is important to try to minimize the likelihood of its causing annoyance. Given the subjectivity of annoyance, the only realistic solution is to provide users with the facility to choose sounds. This would have the additional advantage that users would be able to vary their choice from time to time, further reducing the possibility of annoyance. The problem of offering such a choice is to provide a user interface through which the selection could be made. As it stands, the user input is admirably simple. Allowing sound selection would require either the addition of another input control or the use of the existing controls in some complex and difficult combination (e.g. turning the volume control while holding down the button).

The fact that there is updated information available and about to be presented (in automatic mode) could be cued by another non-speech sound. This might be a better warning than the "You are..." prefix. A short run of notes of rising pitch is found to give an appropriate anticipatory cue to the start of an utterance. Similarly the end of a message could be signalled by a non-speech sound. In natural speech, the intonation usually enables the listener to gauge when the end of a message is approaching, but it is not always possible to provide sufficiently accurate cues when using synthetic speech, particularly for long messages.

A non-speech terminator would avoid this problem, without causing memory problems due to the suffix effect. A short run of notes of falling pitch works well as a terminator. Of course, the use of additional non-speech sounds would introduce further possible sources of annoyance and therefore raises the same issues discussed earlier, such as whether or not users should be able to choose their sounds – or switch them off all together.

7.2.5 Recommendations

Long initial messages, such as example (1), seem inevitable. It cannot be deduced which information the driver needs and so as much as is available must be presented. The structure of the message, based on pauses, does facilitate the reception of the required information.

However, there is scope to improve the *en route* messages, such as example (2). Once on the motorway the first message might be:

(4) [Rising tones] M1 junction 41 southbound. Traffic flowing freely [Falling tones].

At the next transmitter, the message could be reduced to:

(5) [Rising tones] Junction 40. Traffic flowing freely [Falling tones].

The driver already knows that he or she is on the M1 travelling south. The Freeway indicated this in example (4), so even if this route has been taken by mistake the driver will by now be aware of his or her location. To be reminded – at every junction – will quickly become annoying.

If the driver actively requests speech by pressing the button in automatic mode, it would be reasonable to assume that he or she wants full information, in which case the full message would be presented. For example, if the user presses the button after having heard example (5), the following message would be presented:

(6) [Rising tones] M1 junction 40 southbound. Traffic flowing freely [Falling tones].

Such variation in messages would rely on a model of the user – but it could be a very simple one. For example, a rule might be that in composing a message, no information should be included that has already been presented in the previous message. A strict application of that rule would require that example (5), following example (4), be reduced to

(7) [Rising tones] Junction 40 [Falling tones].

but it could be argued that this is entirely appropriate.

When all is well, the message that will be heard most frequently will be "Traffic flowing freely". In automatic mode the driver does not need to hear this every time a different transmitter is passed, but the occurrence of a "beep" provides reassurance that the road ahead is known to be clear. The only problem with this is that the beep sound currently used is somewhat obtrusive and more likely to evoke a startled response than provide reassurance.

It might thus be possible to add a new operational mode as an alternative to automatic mode, in which edited spoken messages of novel information only – as in example (7) – are presented. The usefulness of this mode would, of course, have to be balanced against the increased complexity of adding a further mode – not the least in terms of the user interface.

7.2.6 Summary

Traffic information for drivers is a good application of speech. It delivers useful, detailed information while causing the driver a minimum of distraction. There is some scope for improvement, though:

- replacement of some of the speech by non-speech sounds;
- eliminating the presentation of known information.

This is an application in which the use of speech is very appropriate. The user has a primary task – driving a car – which is safety critical. Therefore any additional information supplied to the driver must be designed to cause minimal disruption. The device described in this section seems to get the balance about right, but it is worth bearing in mind that an increasing number of devices are becoming available that are designed to be used by car drivers. As well as driving-related systems, there are various communication devices. The mobile cellphone is already ubiquitous but various forms of mobile internet terminals are becoming available. Users and designers of such systems should be acutely aware of the possible danger they might present (see Edwards, 1998a).

7.3 The SpeakEasy NT Voicemail System

No matter how unpopular they may be with many users, voicemail systems are a part of modern communication. This section reviews one example system, SpeakEasy NT.[2] Again this is an application that lends itself naturally to a speech-based interface, since the telephone is a speech-based device.

Most people use voicemail systems as answering machines, though the name "voicemail" refers to the fact that it can be used as a form of asynchronous communication. That is to say that the initiator can send a (voice) message that does not have to be answered immediately (as a telephone call does). Instead, the message will be stored and can be picked up at any time by the receiver. However, in this example we will concentrate on the use of the system as an answering machine.

This is not a manual for the use of this system. Therefore the following narrative is not comprehensive. It does not describe all the features of the system, but rather concentrates on interesting aspects of its use of speech.

This voicemail system operates on an internal telephone system, as might be installed within a company that has a central (automated) switchboard. A voicemail box is associated with each telephone extension. Voicemail messages can be sent between extensions connected to the same exchange, but the system will also operate as an answering machine for calls from any telephone, internal or external.

7.3.1 Picking up Messages

The user connects with the system by dialling a telephone number. This may be done from an extension or any other telephone, internal or

---

[2] Voice Integrated Products Ltd, VIP House, 3 Park Place, North Road, Poole, Dorset, UK, BH14 0LY.

external. On dialling the number the connection is instant (i.e. the "phone" does not ring at all). The system announces

Welcome to SpeakEasy NT. Please dial your mailbox number.[3]

The speech uses copy synthesis of a female voice with a neutral accent. It is possible to hear where some of the utterances have been grafted together, but not to the point of being unnatural.

The user enters the number. For security and confidentiality, each user chooses a secret, four-digit PIN number, so this is requested next:

Thank you. Now please dial your PIN number.

There is something of a pause between entering the numbers and the system responding. This can break the flow slightly, but if the user tries to move ahead (e.g. assuming that the mailbox number has been entered correctly and immediately entering the PIN) the system responds with an error message:

I'm sorry, this mailbox number is invalid.

Notice the polite tone; the machine says "please", "thank you" and "I'm sorry". Having entered these numbers correctly, the system announces:

Main menu. There are some new messages for you. To send a message, dial 1. To retrieve your messages, dial 2. For your greeting options, dial 3. For mailbox options dial 4. For your personal groups, dial 5. To transfer elsewhere, dial 6. To leave voicemail dial star.

Naturally the exact content of this message depends on the state of the system. If there are no new messages then this will be signalled, "There are no new messages for you."

The inclusion of the phrase "Main menu" helps the user maintain context. The rest of the utterance is essentially a list – or menu – of options and it has been recorded with appropriate prosody; each of the options has a distinct "hat" pattern, rising on the first half of the sentence

---

[3] It is interesting that the designers have chosen the word "dial". Most telephones no longer have dials. Those that do would not work with this system, which requires the pulse-tone dialling of a keypad telephone, but the word seems to be accepted as the appropriate verb in this context.

("To send a message", etc.) and falling on the instruction ("dial 1"). The final sentence ("To leave voicemail dial star") has a simple, falling, Tone 1 prosody, signalling the end of the list.

All utterances are interruptible. This is an important feature, particularly as the user becomes familiar with the system. A user dialling in to check for messages will quickly hear whether there are any or not and will not have to wait to hear the end of the menu before making a selection from it. In other words, it is necessary to use the start of the next utterance as a cue that the system is ready for the next input, but it is not necessary to wait for all of that utterance. In some systems it may be possible to program sequences of presses into a speed-dial feature, so that the user can connect with the system with just one or two presses.

The assignment of commands to keys in the main menu is a little odd. The announcement "There are some new messages for you." cues the user to deal with new messages. Therefore it might be expected that the first option in the menu would allow the user to hear those messages. The message might seem more natural if it were phrased like this:

> There are some new messages for you. To hear those messages, dial 1. To send a message, dial 2...

Thus the first item in the menu would be associated with the first part of the utterance. With the system as it is, though, a user who presses 2 would hear the following message:

> Retrieval menu. You have 2 new messages and 10 old messages. For new messages dial 1. For old messages dial 2. For the main menu dial star.

The system maintains the context by reminding the user which menu he or she is in, in this case the Retrieval menu. The ordering here is consistent (i.e. the first-named option is associated with button 1). Pressing 1 elicits:

> Voice Message 1. Recorded today at twelve forty three.

The message will then be played. The user can control the playback of the message by pressing keys to "rewind", "fast forward", pause and jump to the end. On completion of the message, the user is prompted:

> To replay this message, dial 1. To erase, dial 2. To respond, dial 3. To retain, dial 4. To play the time stamp, dial 5. To cancel retrieval, dial star.

Option 1 simply causes the message to be replayed. If 2 is pressed, the current message will be deleted, which is confirmed by a simple:

Message erased. This completes your messages. Main menu…

"Responding" in this example refers to sending a return voicemail. If the user chooses to retain the message it will be stored in the system's memory (i.e. it will become an "old message"). Option 5 makes the system speak the time stamp on the message to be repeated, and pressing star takes the user back to the main menu (automatically retaining the message).

7.3.2 Sending Voicemails

Voicemails can be sent to other people on the same system either by selecting option 1 in the main menu or by "responding" to a received message. The user will be prompted:

Please dial the required mailbox or group number.

It is interesting that the term "mailbox number" is used. It is consistent with the view of the system as being based on a mail metaphor, but to many users it is an extension on the telephone network and they are dialling an extension number. Because of this, they may be confused as to whether the mailbox number is something different from the extension number.

Having entered the number, the user will hear the name of the owner of that mailbox – in the owner's voice. The change from the system's voice may be distracting, but is inevitable in a system that uses copy synthesis and is thus incapable of pronouncing arbitrary names. It might be argued that it also provides a degree of personalization in that the sender will hear the (presumably familiar) voice of the intended receiver.

To continue, dial 1. To add another recipient, dial 2. To cancel sending, dial star.

If the sender presses 1:

Please record your message, after the tone, and dial any number when complete.

Having entered a message (and dialled any number) the user can send the message or modify it in various ways (re-recording, appending, editing and so on).

7.3.3 Leaving Messages

The caller to the voicemail system may be connected to it immediately or diverted to it when the telephone has not been answered within a preset number of rings. In either case the caller will hear whatever greeting the user has left. The greeting is recorded by the owner of the extension (mailbox), using option 3 of the main menu. This will be followed by a tone, after which a message may be recorded.

Whatever the quality of the speech design elsewhere in the system, the greeting is one area over which the user has control. In designing a message, the user might like to consider some of the lessons of this book. While issues such as the order of the information require thought and careful planning, it can be assumed that users will automatically apply the appropriate prosody.

The way that an individual uses the voicemail depends on the work they do and their style of working. Most people probably use the voicemail as a simple answering machine. In that case the message they record will probably be a conventional answering-machine-style message such as:

> This is Richard Maxwell. I cannot answer the phone at the moment, but if you leave a message after the tone, I will get back to you as soon as possible.[4]

Such a message might be left on the system for weeks. It may signal that the person is absent from the office at the time of the call – but could equally be used by someone who prefers not to be interrupted by interactive telephone calls and prefers the asynchronous style of voicemail exchanges.

However, some people may have a rather more dynamic style of working so that it is important to refresh their message regularly.

> This is Richard Maxwell. On Thursday 7th January I will be out of the office all morning, but you might be able to catch me in the afternoon. Otherwise you can leave a message after the tone and I will get back to you as soon as possible.

It would be unwise to try to pack much more information into the message. For example, if you are going to be in and out of the office all week,

---

[4] It is beyond the scope of this book to go into any discussion as to the correct identification of the speaker: is it "Richard Maxwell" or "Richard Maxwell's voicemail"?

it is probably better to update the message daily than to try to leave a week's itinerary in one message.

Of course, if there is any more critical information in the message, then the user should be aware of its placement in the message:

> This is Richard Maxwell. I am going to be out of the office all day. However, if you have an urgent need to get me, you can phone me on my mobile. The number is 0777 1235 349.

Putting the number at the end avoids any suffix effects. It should, of course, be broken-up into small groups of digits and read slowly – and possibly repeated, given that the caller cannot hear the message repeated other than by calling again. It might be an idea to design the utterance so as to give the caller more warning that a number is coming, so that they can make preparations to write it down. The user should read the number in an appropriate, natural way, with good pausing and intonation.

Just as the speech is always interruptible, the user can hang up at any time. The system then resets itself in a sensible default state. For example, if the user should hang up during the playback of a message, that message will be retained.

7.3.4 Summary

On the whole, speech is used well in this system. Although it is possible to "hear the joins" in the digitized utterances, they sound sufficiently natural. There is good use of prosody and pausing in the presentation of the information, including lists (menus). The message content is generally well chosen, although there a few that could be improved.

7.4 Design of a Speaking Video Recorder Interface

Whereas driver information systems (as exemplified by the Trafficmaster Freeway) and voicemail systems are inherently suitable applications of speech output, there are other applications in which speech, while not strictly necessary, might have some benefits. In this section we will look at one such application, that of a video recorder timer.

There was a time when people had to make a choice in their social and entertainment lives. If a programme's timing on television clashed with some other event (such as a party) then they had to choose one over the other. However, now that inexpensive video cassette recorders (VCRs) exist, this dilemma no longer exists. The VCR can be programmed so that the required transmission is recorded while the owner is out, to be played back at their convenience.

Programming the VCR correctly, though, can be a challenge. It is suggested that there is a scale of levels of frustration, as follows:

1   To forget that a given programme is on and not set the VCR to record it is mildly annoying.

2   It is slightly more annoying if one remembers to set the recorder, but makes an error in doing so, such that nothing is recorded.

3   Sometimes the recorder is set for the right times – but the wrong channel. To come home in anticipation of watching a favourite programme and find that one has in fact recorded a programme of no interest is rather more annoying.

4   Finally, the most annoying situation of all is to be watching the recorded programme and for it stop suddenly part-way through.

There is scope to design better interfaces for VCR programmers in an effort to minimize the occurrence of these kinds of errors. Manufacturers have tried many approaches, such as the use of VideoPlus codes and on-screen programming interfaces, but it might be appropriate to see whether a speech-based interface might be more successful. Such an interface would have wider application in that it would facilitate the programming of the VCR by blind people.[5] Also such an interface might be accessible over a telephone connection, so that problem (1) in the list above might be addressed; if you have forgotten to set the VCR you phone it up and program it while you are at the party.

---

[5] It might be assumed that recordings of television programmes are of little interest to blind people, but this is not the case. This can be demonstrated by the high take-up of the free television licence that is available to blind people in the UK. The availability of audio description (Lodge, 1995) will only increase this demand.

We will consider only the requirement to program the VCR to record one or more programmes[6] at predetermined times. Also, in the context of this book, we are concerned mainly with the design of the speech output and not with the details of the interaction. It is assumed that there are five input buttons available: TIMER, SELECT, UP, DOWN and CHANGE. These might be part of a standard VCR remote control handset, or, in the case of a telephone-based interface, five of the numerical buttons might be assigned each of these functions.

There are three fundamental operations:

Set   Specify a new timeslot. That is, enter the date, start and stop times and channel of a programme to be recorded.

Check   Read back a timeslot or set of timeslots to ensure they are correct.

Edit   Change one or more of the fields in a timeslot in case an error has been made or the user has changed his or her mind.

The data to be entered consists of:

Slot number   The VCR will accept a sequence of timeslots so that a number of programmes can be recorded in sequence. These are identified by numbers.

Date   The date of the recording.

Channel   The number of the channel on which the programme will be broadcast.

Times   The start and end times of the programme.

---

[6] There is a potentially confusing ambiguity in the language associated with this exercise. In this context the word "programme" may be associated with (a) a television transmission, (b) the act of setting the VCR to record at a preset time, or (c) the list of instructions that represent a schedule of times. The latter two uses of the word are related to the concept of a computer program. The current convention in British English is that this use of the word is spelt "program", while the former use is spelt "programme" (although of course, such spelling differences are irrelevant when the word is presented in speech). We endeavour to avoid ambiguity in this discussion by using the word to refer to a transmission, while using synonyms in the other cases.

All of these data are of type ordinal, according to Zhang's classification (Zhang, 1996). That is to say that there is an order defined. In most cases it is numerical. The only possible exception is the days of the week, since there is no agreed convention as to whether the week starts on a Monday or Sunday – or even Saturday. Thus there is no zero or starting point.

7.4.1 Considerations

The objective is to design an interface optimized for speech-based interaction. However, there are broader usability considerations that must be taken into account.

The interface should be consistent with sources of information. Television listings in newspapers and magazines list the start time of each programme. It is simple therefore to specify the start time of the programme to be recorded, and use the start time of the following programme as the time to terminate the recording.

A variety of different mechanisms could be used to input this kind of data. The data is alphanumeric, so it would be possible (via a keyboard, for example) to enter it in a raw format (e.g. typing the date as "12/12/02" or "12 December 2002"). This could be done very flexibly, allowing the user to choose the format of the data to a large extent (i.e. treating the two versions of the date above as equivalent). However, this would require a full keyboard for input and would also be prone to typing errors.

It can also be observed that all the data is from restricted sets (e.g. there are only 12 months in a year and 60 minutes in an hour). Therefore some form of menu-based input is possible. This is less prone to error and can be achieved with a simple interface.

It is helpful for the interface to use the "language" of the user, but the extent to which that is possible may be constrained by other factors. Also, users vary. For example, some people are familiar and comfortable with the 24-hour clock, so that a time of (say) 1700 hours is both meaningful and unambiguous. However, a simple error others might make is to enter that time for a programme which starts at 7 p.m.

There is certainly scope for customization, allowing the user to input individual preferences. However, it is often observed that most users do not use customization features where they are available. It is usually only advanced, dedicated users who get as far as learning how to implement customizations, and it might be argued that such users are the ones who can probably cope best with interface problems. So, for the most part it is necessary to compromise, and to offer the simplest, broadest interface.

Slot Number

This is simply a way of identifying one slot from another. It can be assigned automatically by the system. Slots do not have to be entered in chronological order and therefore the order of the slot numbers is not significant.

Date

The date may be expressed in different ways. It can be relative, using terms such as "today" and "tomorrow", or it can be absolute, such as 12th December 2002. Relative terms are meaningful in many contexts. "Today" and "tomorrow" are certainly useful, and others such as "a week today" might be, but any more complex ones are likely to be confusing (e.g. "a week on Thursday"). Also some relative terms, as used in conversation, can be ambiguous; does "next Wednesday" refer to the next Wednesday – the soonest occurrence of that day – or the one after that?

Absolute dates may be expressed in a number of formats. They must include a day and a month. In this application, the year will usually be assumed to be the current one, though the facility to specify a date in a different year must be allowed.

Again, the most useful way to specify the day in the near future may be by the day of the week (e.g. Monday); television viewers will often know that a certain programme occurs regularly on a given day. However, days of the week are ambiguous, unlike a date within a month.

There must be consistency between the format used for input and that displayed. For example, if the interface allowed the user to input a day as "Tomorrow", but it was then read back as "13th December" there would be a dissonance. The user might conclude that he or she had made an error in entering the data, or alternatively might have to undertake some complex checking to ensure that tomorrow really is 13th December.

Day numbers in the UK are conventionally expressed as cardinal rather than ordinal numbers (i.e. first, second, third, fourth rather than one, two, three, four). However, most cardinal numbers are formed by adding the "th" suffix to the ordinal number. The high frequency th sound is unlikely to be clearly audible in synthetic speech. Also, the presentation of a number in isolation (i.e. not part of a date) is unnatural in cardinal format.

The format of dates also varies internationally. In the UK, numerical dates are presented in the order day/month/year but in North America the order is month/day/year. This is a fundamental difference, since a date such as 2/3/03 is ambiguous. It is a valid date in either format, but it would be treated as 2nd March in one country and 3rd February in another. A similar (though less hazardous) difference is found with other formats. Conventionally in the UK a date would be expressed as day/month-name, as above (e.g. 2nd March), but in North America the month-name usually comes first (e.g. March 2nd).

These differences are so important that it would be necessary to provide different versions for the UK and American market. In the remainder of this discussion we will consider only the UK version.

Time

As already hinted, alternative time formats are available. The 24-hour clock is unambiguous but unfamiliar to many users. The usual alternative is the use of the suffix am or pm. This is unfortunate because it may lead to suffix effects when presented in speech. For example, the user might forget the time, which was announced at the beginning of the utterance. Alternatively the user might get the wrong part of the day. Having heard the time (11, say), they might not listen for – or might even interrupt – the speech containing the am/pm suffix. Again, consistency is important. If the user has entered a 12-hour time, it must not be read back in 24-hour format.

Written time formats are usually numerical, but in conversation we tend to use terms such as "half-past" and "twenty to". Though these are more colloquial, they are not compatible with written notations of times, as in television listing magazines.

Channel

All televisions have channels identified by numbers. These are mapped onto station names. We will assume that the mapping is known to the system, so that, for example, if the user selects Channel 1, the system can display that as "Channel 1: BBC 1". It must be borne in mind that some users may have a very large number of channels available (perhaps even hundreds of them).

7.4.2 Design

Considering the arguments above, the input would be based entirely on menus. Operations must allow movement up and down the menu – at slow, precise rates as well as fast rates. The other operation would be select. All the menus are circular. For example, in a month menu, January will follow December.

All speech output is interruptible. That is to say that if any button is pressed while speech is being output, that utterance is immediately cut short (as well as the button's function being carried out).

The design is explained by way of an example, as might be presented in the user manual for the device. Design decisions are explained in footnotes.

7.4.3 Example

This recorder allows you to set a timer to record programmes at times in the future when you are not going to be in or perhaps you will be in bed. For the sake of this manual, a programme is a television transmission on a particular channel that starts and ends at a given time. You may arrange for up to 16 such programmes to be recorded automatically by the timer.

To introduce you to setting the timer, we will work through an example. Suppose that you want to record a programme that will be transmitted on Channel 2 (which is BBC 2 on your television) on 28th December, starting at 8:10 p.m. and ending at 8:50.

All of the information is entered through menus. You can move up and down through menu items using the corresponding buttons. As you move through the items they will be spoken. When you hear the item you want, you select it by pressing the SELECT button. If you are not sure which is the current item, you can hear it spoken again by pressing the SPEAK button.

Press the TIMER button on your control. The set will say:

Main menu: There are no programmes scheduled to be recorded. Set timer.[7]

---

[7] Each of the sentences should be spoken with appropriate intonation, and with a pause between them. A suitable intonation pattern for the first two sentences would be Tone 1. The word "no" in the second sentence would be given pitch prominence. The third sentence, "Set Timer", invites the user to select an item from a menu; it could be presented either as a statement (using Tone 1) or as a question (using, e.g. Tone 2).

You are now in a menu. There are two options, and the current one has been announced, "Set timer". You could move down the menu with the DOWN button, but in this case you are on the option you want, so press SELECT. Programmes are entered in slots which are automatically numbered, so the set will tell you

> Slot one.

and put you in a new menu, the Date menu:

> Date: Today.[8]

You do not want to record today, so move down:

> Tomorrow.

Move down again:

> 25.[9]

The menu now consists of dates within the current month. Move down to the required 28th:

> 26, 27, 28.[10]

Press SELECT. You must now select the month, but the default is the current one:

> Month: December

---

[8] All menus are announced by their name and the first (default) entry. There is a pause between the two. The menu could be treated as an alternative question, with the name spoken using Tone 1 intonation and the individual entries spoken using Tone 2. Additionally, the individual menu entries could be presented at successively lower pitches, thus providing the listener with contextual cues (see Section 6.5).

[9] The default starting date will be the current date. That is to say that in this example today is 25th December. This means that a user who prefers not to use "Today" but who prefers to enter the date as a number may still do so.

[10] The timing of the speaking of this list will depend on the user; each number is spoken after a button-press. They are spoken with a neutral tone. Although they form a list, so that a falling pitch might seem appropriate, the system cannot know in advance how long the list will be. Ideally, natural breaks (the last date of a month, for example) might be spoken with a lower pitch.

Press SELECT.[11]

> Channel 1: BBC1.[12]

Move DOWN to Channel 2:

> Channel 2: BBC2

and press SELECT.

> Start time: p.m.[13]

Press SELECT.

> Start hour: four

Press DOWN, repeatedly:

> Five, six, seven, eight.

Press SELECT.

> Start minutes: five.

Press DOWN repeatedly to 10:

> Six, seven, eight, nine, ten.

Press SELECT.

> End time: p.m.[14]

---

[11] Note that there is no mechanism for the entry of a year. All dates are assumed to be in the current or subsequent year. In other words, if the current date is December 2002 and the user enters a date in January, that will be assumed to be January 2003. This is a simple usability choice, but does mean that programmes more than 11 months hence cannot be set to be recorded.

[12] The default is the most recently selected channel.

[13] The default start time is "now". In other words, this example is taking place at 4:05 p.m.

[14] The default end time is the start time.

Press SELECT.

> End hour: eight.

Press SELECT.

> End minutes: ten.

Press and hold DOWN. You will hear a sound like a tape recording being fast forwarded.[15] There will also be a beep marking each ten passed (twenty, thirty and so on). If you release the DOWN button, after three beeps you might hear:

> Forty-four.

Press DOWN repeatedly:

> Forty-five, forty-six, forty-seven, forty-eight, forty-nine, fifty.

Press SELECT.

> Slot one complete.

> Main menu: Set timer.[16]

The timer has been set for one programme. You are back at the Main menu. You can now check the entry you have just made. If you press DOWN now, you will hear:

> Check time slot.

---

[15] This is an interesting melding of speech and non-speech sounds. What is played is really a non-speech sound (it is not possible to hear individual words) but is derived from speech. It is a useful metaphor since most people will be familiar with fast-forwarding a tape recorder. This kind of acceleration is important because there will be some very long menus to be navigated.

[16] There must be a long pause before "Main menu".

If you press SELECT you will hear:

Slot one. Twenty-eighth of December. Channel One: BBC One. Start at eight-ten p.m. End at eight-fifty p.m.[17]

Main menu: Set timer.

Programmes can be changed. The third entry in the main menu is:

Change time slot.

Suppose you have realized that the programme you want to record is actually on Channel 52 and that it ends at 8:55, so you select this option.

Slot one.

Press SELECT.

Twenty-eighth of December.

Press SELECT again.

Channel One: BBC One.

Press CHANGE. Now press and hold DOWN. Release it when you have heard five beeps (representing channels 10, 20, 30, 40 and 50).

Channel Fifty-one: Sky Sports.[18]

Press DOWN again:

Channel Fifty-two: BBC Choice.

---

[17] Each of the sentences should be spoken with appropriate intonation, and with a pause between them, as signalled by the full stops in the transcription. A suitable intonation pattern would be Tone 1.

[18] It is most likely that the menu will have over-shot Channel 50, given the user's reaction time delay.

Press SELECT:

> Start at eight-ten p.m.

Press SELECT:

> End at eight-fifty p.m.

Press CHANGE:

> End hour: eight.

Press SELECT.

> End minutes: fifty.

Press DOWN five times:

> Fifty-one, fifty-two, fifty-three, fifty-four, fifty-five.

Press SELECT. You are back at the main menu:

> Change time slot.

Press DOWN.

> Start timer.

Press SELECT and the timer will be activated to record the programme you have specified.

7.4.4 Implementation

The VCR interface might use digitized or TTS speech. Nearly all of the vocabulary is fixed: numbers, months and so on. Thus recordings of these words could be used. This would have the usual advantages in terms of the quality of the voice attainable. Of course, for the sake of quality, more than one recording of each utterance might be used so that the right intonation can be applied in context. The one item of vocabulary that is not fixed is the channel name. Different people can receive different channels, depending on their facilities (whether they have a digital decoder, satellite dish or whatever). Yet even if the device was loaded with every possible channel name, in the volatile market of entertainment, channels will come and go and be re-named. It would thus be impossible to ensure that a list of channel names loaded in the device was complete. To not speak the channel name (just the number) would be a serious omission; how many people could remember which channel is which from hundreds of possibilities?

This limitation suggests that TTS might be a better alternative. It would provide an unlimited vocabulary, allowing new channel names to be spoken as they arise. Of course, they would be spoken in a mechanical-sounding voice, and might even be mis-pronounced. However, set against that, the synthesizer might be programmed to give better suprasegmental quality than digitized speech. For example, a digitized speech system might have two recordings of numbers, each with a different intonation, but that might not be sufficient. The day of the month would be spoken one way when being read out to confirm the setting of the current time slot (e.g. Tone 1), but if spoken as part of a list (as when selecting the date) its intonation would depend on its place in the list. For example, it might be used as a marker if it is a particular number, such as 1 or 31. Furthermore, the same number might be spoken differently when presented as part of a time than when presented as part of a date. That kind of variation could be achieved with a flexible, well programmed TTS synthesizer.

7.4.5 Summary

This example uses an application that does not naturally suggest a speech-based interface, but it would be interesting to see whether such an interface – if well designed – leads to better, less error-prone operation.

7.5 Conclusions

This chapter has examined several uses of speech in different devices. They all share the same characteristic, though, that good quality is important, not just in terms of the intelligibility of the speech, but also in the choice and ordering of words and the prosodic modulation applied to it.

Future Trends

8.1 Introduction

To speculate about the future is always a hazardous undertaking, because it is so easy to get it wrong and then be held up to ridicule. In the case of technology, the dangers are no less and the examples of getting it wrong abound and yet some people – so-called futurologists – make a career of it. In this chapter we will attempt to look a little way into the future of speech-based devices, but in doing so we acknowledge that we are prepared to be proven wrong.

8.2 Technology

Alan Turing, the pioneer of computer science, proposed a test to determine whether a computer could be regarded as intelligent or not (Turing, 1950). He suggested that if a person could carry out a "conversation" with a computer via a teletypewriter (this test was devised in the 1950s) and could not tell whether the participant at the other end of the link was a computer or a person, then the computer could be said to be intelligent. The requirement here is clearly that the computer must react intelligently: it must produce sensible answers to questions, it should probably pose questions itself at appropriate times, and so on.

Turing predicted that the test would be passed by a computer before the end of the century. Though many people have tried, none quite succeeded within Turing's predicted time, though some have come close. There is an annual competition for the Loebner Prize, which will be awarded to the team that first passes the Turing Test, but which remains unclaimed to date.
(See http://www.loebner.net/Prizef/loebner-prize.html.)

Of course, the use of the teletypewriter was a necessary condition of the test because at that time conversation through speech – in either direction – was impossible. However, it is tempting to suggest that speech synthesis technology will soon reach a stage where it could pass a version of the Turing Test, comparing speech generated by a human or a synthesizer. That it to say that, judging on the sound of the speech alone (not its content), most people would be unable to say whether they were listening to a synthetic or human voice.

Judging on past performance, it is safe to predict that speech technology will continue to develop and improve. The speech sounds at both the segmental and suprasegmental levels will improve. At the same time, some of the research questions raised in this book will no doubt be addressed, so that we can expect there to be many improvements in the technology available.

Another prediction is that speech will cease to be employed mainly for its novelty value, and instead be used in applications where it is genuinely useful, where it has some advantage over alternative forms of communication. There are two areas that are important:

- where other communication channels are not available

- where speech is more natural.

8.3 Speech as an Alternative Channel of Communication

There are a number of situations in which auditory communication is either required or desirable. One is as part of any task that requires the operator's full visual attention, but in which it is desirable or necessary to present additional information to the operator. To add information to the visual display might clutter it, making it more difficult to interpret and/or distracting attention from the primary task. The obvious example is driving a car or other vehicle, and this is certainly a task in which speech will increasingly be used.

It may be that the extra information that is to be presented aurally is relevant to the driving task, such as the traffic reports produced by the Trafficmaster, or directions to the destination. This kind of use seems legitimate and sensible. The operator (the driver in this case) is heavily loaded with (visual) information and so further information that is germane to the main task should be presented through another sensory channel. If it is done in an appropriate manner, it should improve the efficiency and security of the main task. For example, a driver who receives spoken directions to a required street can maintain full visual attention to steering the car rather than looking around for the name on street signs.

Increasingly, though, there is a temptation for drivers to undertake other tasks while driving. We are approaching the situation where the car is an extension of the office. Already drivers keep up with their telephone communication while driving and it is now also possible to do other jobs that used to be confined to the office, such as reading and writing emails, surfing the web and so on. While speech technology will facilitate such interaction, it is not advocated by the authors. Any task that distracts the driver's attention from the primary task of driving is potentially dangerous. A study in Canada (Redelmeier and Tibshirani, 1997) has demonstrated that the risk of having a car accident while using a telephone is comparable to the risk arising from consumption of alcohol. Furthermore, the dangers are similar whether the telephone in use is of a hands-free design or not. In other words, the risk is associated with the verbal task in which the driver is engaged, and not necessarily with the physical manipulation of the telephone handset.

Ignoring or ignorant of these facts, manufacturers are already making available a range of in-car internet terminals. They often make a selling point of the fact that the device is speech-based and therefore, they claim, safe to use while driving. This seems unlikely, and research is urgently required to establish the facts, after which it may be necessary to introduce legislation to determine what devices can and cannot be used by drivers.

Further discussion of the potential perils of driving while interacting with the internet can be found in Edwards (1998a). It seems likely, however, that such warnings are crying in the wilderness, judging by the amount of attention that has been paid to the dangers of telephone use while driving. It is therefore probably another safe prediction that the number and range of speech-based devices used in cars will increase quite rapidly in the near future.

Cars are not the only means of transport, however, and speech will have its place to play in other mobile applications. People still walk – both indoors and outdoors – and sometimes they like to be kept in touch with the wider world while walking. Already there is convergence between the telephone, the internet terminal and the portable hi-fi. Experimental systems, such as those developed by Sawhney and Schmandt (1999) and Mynatt et al. (1997) take this a step further and are likely to lead to powerful mobile communication devices that rely heavily on speech.

The information that might be delivered on such a device is almost unlimited. It may be information germane to the current task, such as directions to one's destination (Loomis et al., 1993), or external communications that the user wants to maintain, such as emails, stock market prices, news and so on. Experiments have also been carried out to examine the value of speech-based communication as an aid to people engaged in various activities. Baber et al. (1999) considered the use of speech by paramedics, who spend much of their time engaged in intensive manual tasks (treating patients) and might find it useful to be able to communicate through speech with another person (e.g. a doctor) or a computer (perhaps containing a database of patients' records).

8.4 Applications for Users with Special Needs

In all of the above examples, speech is an appropriate choice because other channels of communication are already heavily loaded. There are, of course, instances where other channels are not available – because the person in question has a disability. In particular, blind people do not have access to visual modes of communication. All that has been said above applies equally to the blind user, except that in some cases the needs are more extreme because the visual channel is completely unavailable.

As noted in Chapter 1, speech is already widely used in systems for blind people. It is popular because it is cheap and requires little training (unlike Braille). Screen readers allow almost all of the functions involved in using a GUI-based operating system to be performed using the keyboard and synthetic speech (in place of the mouse and visual display).

However, the level of access provided by screen-readers and synthetic speech is not as good as that available to a sighted person using a visual display. Many applications are all but impossible to adapt for speech output because they rely heavily on images, diagrams, etc. Graphics and imaging software are obvious examples, but many other types of software may cause problems too, such as those used in planning, modelling, simulation, and similar tasks. Even software that does not use diagrams or images may cause problems if it relies on visual organization of material. For example, the spatial organization of information in columns and rows on a spreadsheet makes the relationships between the various items of data clear to sighted users, but it is not easy to convey the same relationships to a blind user.

A more fundamental problem is that speech is an inherently slow medium compared with text. As Barry Arons has pointed out, "It is faster to speak than it is to write or type, however it is slower to listen than it is to read" (Arons, 1993). Thus the blind user who has no option but to access text through speech is at a significant disadvantage compared with the sighted user who can rapidly skim through visually presented text.

Another problem is that speech is transient, and once an utterance has ended it has to be stored in the listener's memory (which, as we saw in Chapter 3, has only a limited capacity). By contrast, text can remain visible on a screen for as long as necessary, allowing a (sighted) person to access it repeatedly without having to store it in memory first. Thus the screen acts as a form of external memory (see Section 6.1), making it easier for the user to absorb the information contained in the text, to make comparisons between various items and to make decisions based on the data. However, it leaves those who cannot use a visual display – for whatever reason – at a significant disadvantage. For example, an experiment conducted by the US Air Force compared subjects' ability to respond to emergency messages presented either on screen or via synthetic speech. The results showed that the subjects who received the messages via speech responded more slowly than the subjects who received the visual messages, and also had more difficulty keeping track of the changing situation (Robinson and Eberts, 1987).

There are no simple solutions to these problems, but in the future we can expect to see intelligent adaptations that overcome them in many ways. At present, for example, screen-readers generally convert text on the screen directly into speech. However, as we saw in Chapter 4, spoken language differs in many respects from written language, and the format used to convey a piece of information as text may not be the most appropriate or efficient for speech. It may be possible to overcome this problem using intelligent screen-readers that employ Natural Language Processing (NLP) techniques. Such a system would be able to "understand" the content of a message and rephrase it in a more speech-friendly format.

Spatial sound might also be used to convey some of the information encoded in the layout of printed and screen text. In the Maths project, for example, polynomial equations were presented such that each spoken term appeared to emanate from a different position around the listener (Stevens, 1996). It was found that this greatly assisted the listener in recalling and thinking about an equation. A similar approach could be used to convey some of the spatial organization found in spreadsheets, databases, etc. Previous attempts to use spatial sound in this way have produced encouraging results, but their appeal has been limited by the cost and complexity of the necessary hardware. However, it will soon be possible to deliver convincing spatial sound over headphones (see Section 8.5), and to do so at reasonable cost. Once this happens, we can expect to see widespread use of spatial sound to convey additional information to blind users.

The needs of someone with partial sight (visual impairment) are different from those of a blind person. The visual channel is not completely excluded, and in practice most partially sighted people wish to make as much use of the sight they have as possible, rather than resort to non-visual communication. Therefore they tend to use technology that enhances their visual ability (such as screen-magnifiers) in preference to devices that are entirely non-visual.

Nevertheless, partially sighted users may agree to use a device that has a non-visual channel, especially if non-visual communication channels (such as speech) become widely accepted among other computer users. Therefore we may see the introduction of devices that cater for both speech and enhanced vision and allow a high degree of configuration to suit individual needs.

Opinions differ as to whether illiteracy is a disability. However, it is undoubtedly the case that not being able to read is a severe disadvantage in modern society. Someone who cannot read can have material read to them by a machine. This may be literal – a speech synthesizer attached to a scanner so that books and other printed material can be read – or it may be an alternative to printed forms of communication. For example, a talking bus timetable is accessible to anyone who cannot read a printed version, for whatever reason.

8.5 Speech and Mobile Devices

Speech is an attractive channel in mobile devices because of the portability of speech output; all that is needed is a loudspeaker, which can be quite small. This opens up many possibilities since miniaturization is nowadays limited more by interaction facilities – such as screens and keyboards – than by technical issues.

Until recently it was the case that the more computing power one needed, the larger the computer one had to buy. If one required something that was portable, then one accepted that it would have less power than a physically larger machine. However, this is no longer true, and it is essentially possible to get as much power as you are likely to need for any practical application in a package as small as you want. This means that other factors now determine how big a device will be.

An example is the telephone, which cannot be made significantly smaller as long as it needs to have a keypad for the entry of numbers and text – at least one that the average user can operate with his or her fingers. The visual output of any device is constrained by the size of the screen. Again, the screens on mobile phones well illustrate the limitations imposed by miniaturization.

Sound output (including speech) does not have any of these size limitations. For speech purposes, the sound quality from small speakers is sufficient. This portability is another reason we can expect to see greater use of speech output in the increasing number of mobile and wearable devices that we are going to see in the (near) future.

Another option is to use headphones. These are good acoustically. At one time they might have caused some problems aesthetically, because it was not socially acceptable to wear headphones in public. However, the advent of the portable hi-fi (pioneered by Sony with the Walkman) has turned that around, so that it is quite common to see people wearing headphones of all shapes and sizes in the street. There are other problems with headphones, though, in that they tend to cut out external, real-world sounds. This can be isolating and dangerous. Several devices are available which attempt to capture the best of both worlds. These usually consist of speakers that are in some way worn near the ears but do not cover them.

Another technology exploited in these mobile devices is that of three-dimensional sound spatialization – the processing of the sounds to make them appear to come from different points in the space around the listener's head. Ideally this should be linked to some form of head tracking. On hearing a sound of interest, it is a natural reaction to turn towards it so as to hear it better. However, this does not work when using headphones because they stay in the same position relative to the listener's head, causing the apparent source of the sound to move too. Head-tracking offers a potential solution to this problem, allowing the system to generate signals that correctly reflect the position and angle of the listener's head at all times. Head-tracking technology exists (see, for instance, the Polhemus tracking products at www.polhemus.com), but is as yet far from perfect. This is just one of the technical challenges that needs to be overcome in order to make this technology really useful.

8.6 Avatars

One of the first automatic speech-based information systems was the speaking clock. Being based on the telephone, speech is the natural medium. The original clock in the UK was based on recordings of a female human voice and each individual time in 10-second intervals over 24 hours had been recorded. Subsequently it has been possible to use copy synthesis, whereby the individual components of the time can be stitched together seamlessly – and a sponsor's advertisement inserted.

On the telephone all voices are disembodied, and the speaking clock requires no interaction with the caller. However, many people find telephone interactions with machines uncomfortable. This is evident in the problems some people have in using voicemail systems, particularly in knowing how to address a machine. Does one talk to it as if it is the person whose voice one has just heard, even though one knows they are not there, or does one address the machine as a third party? "Will you tell … when she gets in …" hardly seems an appropriate way to talk to an inanimate machine.

So, it may be that people will be more comfortable interacting with a machine if it behaves more like a person. It is possible to add a human façade to synthetic speech in the form of a visual animation of a person, often referred to as an avatar.

Simple, one-way delivery of information can be achieved quite well with such systems. The first application was in the presentation of news, the best-known example being Ananova (http://www.ananova.com). The role of a newsreader is surely defined by the title: one who reads out the news. It can be argued that human traits are undesirable in this role and that subjective input such as emotional reaction to the material being presented should be avoided. Thus this role seems well suited to a machine that can be given a script and will read it.

However, this raises a question: why should there be any need to pretend that a person is involved by giving the synthetic speech a visual embodiment? Part of the answer, perhaps, is that people have certain social reactions – they engage better with a humanized representation and are more likely to believe what it says. In addition, the representation of the figure adds the further channel of body language, the facial expressions and gestures. This should – if properly implemented – lead to better, less ambiguous communication.

Newsreading is one-directional communication – delivery of information. However, in the future it may be possible for simulated people to engage in dialogue with real people. Furthermore, using speech recognition, it is even possible that the dialogue might be entirely spoken – in both directions. Of course, the hardest aspect of this task will be to simulate what goes on inside a person, their thinking and intelligence.

There are many roles in which it has previously been assumed that it was obligatory to use a person to interact with customers, such as talking with people and dispensing advice. Providing that sort of cover in office hours is expensive; doing it 24-hours a day may be prohibitive. At the time of writing (2002), such systems are on the point of becoming a commercial reality. Their success and degree of acceptance will depend very much on how well they succeed in simulating human interaction.

Any device that uses speech input is very much reliant on the quality of the speech recognition. How well does the system pick out the words that the person has spoken? In this kind of application, the recognition is particularly difficult because it has to work with anybody; it cannot be trained to the individual and has to cope with different voices, accents and all the variation in human speech. And that is the easy part of the problem. If a system is going to interact conversationally, it must at some level understand the utterance. It is not enough for a speech recognizer to identify all the words of the utterance 100% correctly – the system must extract the meaning too. We have already seen many instances in this book of the potential ambiguity of spoken language. A favourite example is the question "Can you tell me the time of the next bus?". It takes a level of insight to recognize that the expected answer to that question is a time – and not simply "Yes".

Most previous attempts to construct such systems have relied on key-word spotting. The system picks out words that have been recognized (with a fairly high level of confidence) from the utterance, and these are then matched, using templates, with attached standard responses. Such a system might work quite well with the above example, matching the words "time", "next" and "bus", ignoring the polite but irrelevant decorations ("can you tell me …") and producing an appropriate response. One will not always be so lucky, though; spotting the wrong keywords or attaching the wrong significance to them may sometimes cause amusement but is more likely to produce frustration or anger. Suppose the system latched on to the word "time" in "Can you tell me the time of the next bus?" and responded "The time now is 12:11". The customer might become very annoyed at being told something he or she already knows by a "dumb machine".

This kind of frustration may be avoided by using more sophisticated systems that attempt real understanding of their input. Such systems rely on some form of Natural Language Processing, and should be capable of building some form of representation of the meaning of an utterance, then responding appropriately (see http://www.lexicle.co.uk, for instance).

It might seem that such avatars could be used in the ultimate Turing test, and that an avatar could look and sound so much like a real person that the user would be fooled into thinking that they are interacting with a person. However, there may be a danger in that – one which brings us back to the original idea of the test. What if the avatar looks and sounds like a person, but does not think like one? The user might reasonably assume that since the avatar looks and sounds like a person, it thinks like a person too. Such high expectations are almost certain to lead to disappointment and frustration.

It might be better to retain a degree of artificiality in the representation of a person, just sufficient to remind the user that they are dealing with a machine and should not expect too much of it. They may be more tolerant of mistakes from something that is obviously a "dumb machine" than they would be from what seems to all intents and purposes to be a person. The artificiality could be achieved by careful programming, or simply by using a less-than-perfect speech synthesizer.

Despite the obvious challenges, the motivation to achieve a good level of artificial interaction is strong. People are expensive to employ. They can be unreliable. They may become ill or discontented with their working conditions. The role of people has already been greatly reduced in industries where robots and computers have been able to replace them with great cost savings. Time will tell how effective and popular such interaction systems will be, but it seems inevitable that they will be used increasingly.

8.7 Unsolved Problems and Issues

There is clearly much scope for further research that will lead to improvements in speech design. Some of the technological issues have been discussed above, but more research is also needed into the way people use language and respond to speech and other sounds.

Any system that interacts with people is likely to be better if it incorporates a model or models of the user, and systems will improve as they make better use of such models. For example, much reference has been made to the distinction between new and old information. We can observe how this distinction influences the way people speak, but if we want to capture and represent this in mechanical dialogues then we need models of information and of its retention and decay in human memory. As pointed out in the example in Section 7.2.5, such models need not be very complex in order to be useful. In the future we can expect to see the development of progressively more and more sophisticated models, allowing interactive systems to respond with much of the flexibility of human beings.

Another area in which more research is needed is the ability of listeners to handle multiple sounds presented simultaneously. As pointed out in Section 3.1, the ability of people to successfully extract information from multiple simultaneous sound sources is often underestimated. It is often claimed that sound is a serial medium, but this is not necessarily true.

When multiple sources of sound exist, the brain copes with them by dividing them into streams. A stream is a set of sounds that are perceived to belong together. There are a number of characteristics that will tend to collect sounds into a stream. These include:

Spatial proximity	Two (or more) sounds emanating from the same spatial area
Temporal proximity	Sounds that occur simultaneously or within a short period of time

147

Timbral similarity	Sounds with similar timbres. For instance, the string section of an orchestra may form one stream.
Rhythm	Sounds with similar rhythms will tend to form a stream – and conversely sounds with different rhythms may be perceived as belonging to different streams. Note that this is related to temporal proximity.

The more of these properties different sounds share, the more likely they are to be perceived as a stream.

One implication of auditory streaming is that in most situations it is possible to construct at least two auditory streams of speech and non-speech sounds. This reinforces the separate cognitive processing of speech and non-speech sounds and so increases the amount of information that can be presented at any time.

In dealing with auditory output that is speech alone, the possibilities for exploiting streaming are reduced. The timbre of one voice is much like the timbre of another. Nevertheless, it is possible to create different speech streams using spatial separation alone. For example it has been observed (Begault and Erbe, 1994) that helicopter pilots need to monitor multiple radio channels (as many as four) but that they can do so much more efficiently if the channels are separated spatially.

In the natural world, sounds are perceived as coming from different directions because their sources are physically separated. In an artificial world, such as a helicopter cockpit, in which sounds are generated by loudspeakers (probably within headphones), this kind of spatial separation can still be achieved artificially. Techniques have been developed whereby sounds to be presented over a pair of speakers or headphones are processed in such a way as to generate the illusion of coming from different points in space, all around the listener.

There are still some problems to be tackled, however, before spatialized sound can become really useful. One problem is that of delivering appropriate signals to each of the listener's ears while taking into account changes in the listener's location and head position, etc. This problem may be overcome through the use of head-tracking, once the problems with this technology have been solved (see Section 8.5).

Another problem with spatialized audio is caused by the fact that individuals vary enormously in their ability to localize sounds. The reasons for this are not entirely understood, but probably have to do with physical differences such as the size and shape of the pinnae (the visible part of the ear on the sides of the head) as well as the size and shape of the head, shoulders, etc. These differences can be measured and captured using a mathematical representation called the Head-Related Transfer Function, or HRTF. To achieve optimal spatialization, the system should be programmed with the individual's HRTF. However, in most applications this is impractical, not least because measuring the HRTF is a complex task. Thus, most current systems are programmed with an "average" HRTF. As a result, the accuracy of the spatialization heard by a particular listener depends, to a large extent, on how much that listener's HRTF differs from the average.

This is another problem that remains to be tackled. Who knows, in the future we may carry our personal HRTF around with us, along with our National Insurance number and other individual data on some form of smart card?

Another phenomenon, related to streaming, is attention. As with streaming, there is often an assumption that – no matter how many streams we can perceive – we can only attend to one of them at a time. Again, however, this assumption is not entirely correct. This is illustrated by the Cocktail Party Effect. This is the effect whereby a person may be in a busy room, engaged in a conversation to which they are giving their full attention and surrounded by a hubbub of noise, yet if someone says their name across the room, they will hear it and have their attention diverted. In other words, though the conscious attention is directed at the conversation, subconsciously their brain is still processing the other sounds around them. This effect is discussed in much greater detail in ten Hoopen (1996). Practical attempts to exploit this effect in user interfaces have so far proved disappointing, but this will almost certainly change as spatial sound systems improve and as the hearing mechanisms underlying the effect become better understood.

8.8 Conclusions

We are likely to see an increase in the number of devices using speech output. This is partly driven by the technology: we do it because we can (and well), but also because new applications are becoming apparent in which the auditory channel is the appropriate one for the delivery of information. There is a certain degree of resistance to the use of speech when communicating with machines, possibly fuelled by the introduction of badly designed devices. An obvious example is the talking car released by a British manufacturer some years ago. Anecdotal evidence suggests that most owners were quickly driven to find a way of disabling the speech, and it was not long before the manufacturer dropped the feature. Had an analysis been carried out that took into account the issues raised in this book, it might well have become apparent where the design errors were, allowing the system to be designed so that it would have been both acceptable and useful. The error was not in including a speech channel; it was in its design.

Appendix A: List of Homophones

Homophones are words that sound the same but have different meanings. They are usually spelt differently, so that when written they are clearly distinguishable, but in a speech-based interface they have the potential to cause ambiguity and confusion and are best avoided. It is worth consulting this list when designing spoken utterances as it is easy to become blinkered, thinking only of the particular meaning one has in mind and forgetting that a homophone might exist.

The following list is based on Alan Cooper's Homonym List (http://www.cooper.com/alan/homonym_list.html), and is used here with his permission. The original list attempts to be comprehensive, but this one is rather more selective and has been edited to include words that seem more likely to occur in speech-based devices. It has also been modified to reflect British pronunciations and spellings, and includes a number of words that are not strict homophones but are close enough in pronunciation to cause confusion.

A

acts	things done
axe	chopping tool
affect	to change
effect	result
air	*see:* err
aisle	*see:* I'll
allowed	permitted
aloud	spoken
altar	raised centre of worship
alter	to change
ant	insect
aunt	parent's sister
ascent	the climb
assent	to agree
ate	past tense of eat
eight	8
aught	anything
ought	should
aural	of hearing
oral	of the mouth

B

ball	playful orb
bawl	to cry
band	a group
banned	forbidden

bare	naked	bolder	more courageous
bear	wild ursine	boulder	large rock
baron	minor royalty	born	brought into life
barren	unable to bear children	borne	past participle of bear
berry	small fruit	bourn	a small stream or
bury	to take under		boundary
base	foundation	bough	tree branch
bass	the lowest musical	bow	front of a ship;
	pitch or range		respectful bend
bases	plural of base	buoy	navigational aid
basis	principal constituent	boy	male child
	of anything	brake	stopping device
basses	many four-stringed	break	to split apart
	guitars	breach	to break through
be	to exist	breech	the back part
bee	insect		
beat	to hit	bread	a loaf
beet	edible red root	bred	past tense of breed
berth	anchorage	brewed	fermented
birth	your method of arrival	brood	family
bight	middle of a rope	bridal	pertaining to brides
bite	a mouthful	bridle	horse's headgear
byte	eight bits	broach	to raise a subject
billed	has a bill	brooch	an ornament fastened
build	to construct		to clothes
blew	past tense of blow	buy	to purchase
blue	colour of California sky	by	near
boar	wild pig	bye	farewell
Boer	a South African of		
	Dutch descent	**C**	
boor	tasteless buffoon	ceiling	*see:* sealing
bore	not interesting		
board	a plank	**E**	
bored	not interested		
bold	brave	effect	*see:* affect
bowled	knocked over	eight	*see:* ate

elicit	to draw out
illicit	unlawful
ere	eventually
err	to make a mistake
e'er	contraction of "ever"
air	gas we breathe
heir	one who will inherit
ewe	*see:* yew

F

facts	objective things
fax	image transmission technology
faint	pass out
feint	a weak, misdirected attack to confuse the enemy
fair	even-handed
fare	payment
feat	an accomplishment
feet	look down
find	to locate
fined	to have to pay a parking ticket
finish	to complete
Finnish	from Finland
fir	evergreen tree
fur	animal hair
furr	to separate with strips of wood
flea	parasitic insect
flee	to run away
flour	powdered grain
flower	a bloom

for	in place of
fore	in front
four	number after three
foreword	introduction to a book
forward	the facing direction
foul	grossly offensive to the senses
fowl	domestic hen or rooster
frees	releases
freeze	very cold
frieze	a wall decoration

G

genes	a chromosome
jeans	cotton twill trousers
gild	to coat with gold
gilled	having gills
guild	a craft society
gilt	gold-plated
guilt	culpable
gorilla	large ape
guerrilla	irregular soldier
grate	a lattice
great	extremely good
grease	lubricant
Greece	Mediterranean country
grill	to sear cook
grille	an iron gate or door
groan	reaction to hearing a pun
grown	has become larger
guessed	past tense of guess
guest	a visitor

153

H

hair	grows from your head
hare	large rabbit
hall	a large room
haul	to carry
hangar	garage for aeroplanes
hanger	from which things hang
hear	to listen
here	at this location
heard	listened to
herd	a group of ruminants
heir	*see:* err
heroin	narcotic
heroine	female hero
hold	to grip
holed	full of holes
hole	round opening
whole	entirety
hour	sixty minutes
our	possessed by us

I

idle	not working
idol	object of worship
illicit	*see:* elicit
I'll	contraction of "I will"
isle	island
aisle	walkway
incite	to provoke
insight	understanding
innocence	a state without guilt
innocents	more than one innocent

it's	contraction of "it is"
its	possessive pronoun

J

jeans	*see:* genes

K

know	to possess knowledge
no	negation
knows	*see:* noes

L

lead	heavy metal
led	guided
leak	accidental escape of liquid
leek	variety of onion
lessen	to reduce
lesson	a segment of learning
loan	allow to borrow
lone	by itself
loch	a lake
lock	a security device

M

made	accomplished
maid	young woman
mail	postal delivery
male	masculine person
maize	corn
maze	puzzle
manner	method
manor	lord's house
marshal	to gather
martial	warlike

massed	grouped together
mast	sail pole
meat	animal flesh
meet	to connect
mete	a boundary
medal	an award
meddle	to interfere
mince	chop finely
mints	aromatic sweets
mind	thinking unit
mined	looked for ore
miner	one who digs
minor	small
missed	not hit
mist	fog
moan	to groan
mown	the lawn is freshly cut
mode	condition
mowed	a lawn in a well-trimmed condition
moor	swampy coastland; to anchor
more	additional
morning	AM
mourning	remembering the dead
muscle	fibrous, contracting tissue
mussel	a bivalve mollusc

N

naval	pertaining to ships and the sea
navel	pertaining to the belly button

no	*see:* know
noes	"The noes have it…"
nose	"Plain as the nose on your face…"
knows	"Only the shadow knows…"
none	not one
nun	woman of God
nose	*see:* noes

O

oar	boat propulsion system
or	alternative
ore	mineral-laden dirt
one	singularity
won	victorious
oral	*see:* aural
ordinance	a decree
ordnance	artillery
ought	*see:* aught
our	*see:* hour

P

packed	placed in a container
pact	agreement
pail	bucket
pale	light coloured
pain	it hurts
pane	a single panel of glass
pair	a set of two
pare	cutting down
pear	bottom-heavy fruit
passed	approved; moved on
past	before now

patience	being willing to wait
patients	hospital residents
pause	hesitate
paws	animal feet
peace	what hippies want
piece	morsel
peak	mountain top
peek	secret look
pique	ruffled pride
pedal	foot control
peddle	to sell
peer	an equal (a captain at sea has no peer)
pier	wharf (a captain at sea has no pier)
pi	3.1416
pie	good eating
place	a location
plaice	a flounder
plain	not fancy
plane	a surface
pleas	cries for help
please	good manners
pole	big stick
poll	a voting
poor	no money
pore	careful study; microscopic hole
pour	to flow freely
praise	to commend
prays	worships God
preys	hunts
precedence	priority
precedents	established course of action
presidents	commanders-in-chief

presence	the state of being present
presents	what Santa brings
pride	ego
pryed	opened
pries	wedging open
prize	the reward
principal	head of school
principle	causative force

Q

quarts	several fourths-of-gallons
quartz	crystalline rock

R

racket	illegal money-making scheme
racquet	woven bat for tennis
rain	precipitation
reign	sovereign rule
rein	horse's steering wheel
raise	elevate
rays	thin beams of light
raze	to tear down completely
rapped	knocked sharply
rapt	spellbound
wrapped	encased in cloth
read	having knowledge from reading
red	a primary colour
rest	stop working
wrest	take away

retch	call Ralph on the porcelain telephone
wretch	a ragamuffin
review	a general survey or assessment
revue	a series of theatrical sketches or songs
right	correct
rite	ritual
wright	a maker
write	to inscribe
ring	circle around your finger
wring	twisting
road	a broad trail
rode	past tense of ride
rowed	to propel a boat by oars
role	part to play
roll	rotate
root	subterranean part of a plant
route	path of travel
rose	pretty flower
rows	linear arrangement
rote	by memory
wrote	has written

S

sail	wind powered water travel
sale	the act of selling
saver	one who saves
savour	to relish a taste
scene	visual location
seen	past tense of saw
scull	rowing motion
skull	head bone
sea	ocean
see	to look
sealing	closing
ceiling	upper surface of room
seam	row of stitches
seem	appears
seas	oceans
sees	looks
seize	to grab
sects	religious factions
sex	if you have to ask, you're too young
sew	needle and thread
so	in the manner shown
sol	musical note
sow	broadcasting seeds
shall	is allowed
shell	aquatic exoskeleton
shear	to cut or wrench
sheer	thin; abrupt turn
sign	displayed board bearing information
sine	reciprocal of the cosecant
slay	kill
sleigh	snow carriage
sleight	cunning skill
slight	not much
soar	fly
sore	hurt
soared	to have sailed through the air
sword	long fighting blade

solace	comfort
soulless	lacking a soul
sole	only
soul	immortal part of a person
some	a few
sum	result of addition
son	male child
sun	star
soot	black residue of burning
suit	clothes
stair	a step
stare	look intently
stake	wooden pole
steak	slice of meat
stationary	not moving
stationery	writing paper
steal	take unlawfully
steel	iron alloy
storey	the horizontal divisions of a building
story	a narrative tale
straight	not crooked
strait	narrow waterway
suede	split leather
swayed	curved; convinced
suite	ensemble
sweet	sugary
summary	precis
summery	like summer
sundae	ice cream with syrup on it
Sunday	first day of the week

T

tacks	small nails
tax	governmental tithe
tail	spinal appendage
tale	story
tare	allowance for the weight of packing materials
tear	to rip
taught	past tense of teach
taut	stretched tight
tea	herbal infusion
tee	golf ball prop
team	a group working together
teem	to swarm
tear	eyeball lubricant
tier	a horizontal row
teas	more than one herbal infusion
tease	tantalize
tees	more than one tee
tense	nervous
tents	more than one temporary shelter
their	belonging to them
there	a place
they're	contraction of "they are"
threw	to propel by hand
through	from end to end
throes	spasms of pain
throws	discharging through the air
throne	the royal seat
thrown	was hurled

tide	periodic ebb and flow of oceans	Wales	Western division of UK
tied	passed tense of tie	whales	a pod of ocean mammals
to	towards	war	large scale armed conflict
too	also		
two	a couple	wore	past tense of wear
toad	frog	ware	merchandize
toed	having toes	wear	attire
towed	pulled ahead	where	a place
toe	forepart of the foot	way	path or direction
tow	to pull ahead	weigh	to measure weight
		whey	watery part of milk
told	what was spoken	weak	not strong
tolled	a bell was rung	week	seven days
tracked	having tracks	weather	meteorological conditions
tract	a plot of land	wether	a castrated ram
trussed	tied up	whether	if it be the case
trust	faith	wet	watery
		whet	prime

V

vain	worthless
vane	flat piece moving with the air
vein	blood vessel
verses	paragraphs
versus	against

W

waist	between ribs and hips
waste	make ill use of
wait	remain in readiness
weight	an amount of heaviness
waive	give up rights
wave	undulating motion

whined	past tense of whine
wind	what you do to a clockwork
wined	drank well of spirits
who's	contraction of "who is"
whose	belonging to whom
whole	*see:* hole
won	*see:* one
wood	what trees are made of
would	will do
wrapped	*see:* rapped

wrest	*see:* rest
wretch	*see:* retch
wright	*see:* right
write	*see:* right
wring	*see:* ring
wrote	*see:* rote

Y

yew	a type of tree
you	the second person
ewe	female sheep
yoke	oxen harness
yolk	yellow egg centre
yore	the past
you're	contraction of "you are"
your	belonging to you

Appendix B: Words with More than One Meaning

The words listed below can take different meanings depending upon the context in which they are used.

Many English words can take several related meanings and function as more than one part of language without a change in the way they are spoken. Words which can be used as different parts of language but refer to the same object or function (for example camp, which can be used as either a verb or a noun) are not included in this list since they pose few problems in the design of speech dialogues. Provided a clause is correctly structured, the way in which the word is being used will be clear to the listener.

However, where a word can take more than one meaning while functioning as the same part of language (for example jet which, when used as a noun, can mean either a stream of liquid or an aircraft) it must be used with care in order to avoid ambiguity.

The following list contains a selection of such words, but is not exhaustive.

Word	Meanings
Air	gaseous mixture, melody
Bark	outer sheath of tree trunk, sound made by animal (e.g. dog), abrade
Bill	demand for money, act of parliament, beak of web-footed bird
Deal	fir or pine wood, business agreement, distribution of playing cards or other items
Die	numbered cube used in games of chance, mould used to stamp shape in metal, cease living
File	instrument used to shape or smooth materials, collection of papers or records, line of people or objects
Fly	move through the air, run away, two-winged insect
Jet	stream of liquid, black lignite, aircraft
Jig	lively tune or dance, device for holding work-piece in machine tool

Joint	junction between two parts, portion of animal prepared as food, in common
Just	merely, precisely, in accordance with justice
Keen	sharp-edged, enthusiastic
Kit	personal effects, equipment or clothing needed for particular task, set of components
Lace	fine fabric, cord used for fastening shoes, etc., act of fastening using cord
Lap	front of thighs of a seated person, overhanging edge, e.g. of floorboard, single turn around, e.g. race track, cable reel, etc.
Left	remaining, opposite direction to right
Let	hinder or obstruct, allow or enable, hire
Lie	make a false statement, adopt a horizontal position, shape or pattern or distribution (e.g. of land)
Lock	secure fastening, portion of hair
Mass	celebration of the Eucharist, coherent body of matter
Match	competitive endeavour, short piece of wood with combustible tip, equal or complementary
Mean	stingy, equidistant from two extremes, have as purpose
Mine	excavation in earth, explosive device, statement of possession
Mould	fungal growth, pattern or template, give shape to
Neat	tidy, undiluted
Page	leaf of book, boy employed as servant, summon
Palm	inner surface of hand, tropical tree
Peer	one who is equal in some respect, noble person, look intently
Pen	writing instrument, enclosure
Pole	stick, magnetic pole, native of Poland
Quarry	place from which stone is extracted, object of hunt
Race	ethnic group, competition by speed, strong current
Rail	abuse or react strongly against, enclose with rails, bars placed horizontally and/or in continuous series
Rank	line or queue (e.g. of taxis), position within hierarchy, loathsome, corrupt, sort by some criterion
Rear	breed, cultivate, rise up, hindmost part
Right	correct, good, opposite of left, entitlement
Sack	dismiss from employment, pillage, large bag of coarse fabric
Sage	herb, wise person

Saw	observed, cut using a to-and-fro motion, device for cutting, old saying
Scale	horny plate forming skin of fish or reptile, graduated continuum against which value is measured, device for measuring weight, sequence of musical notes
Shy	move away suddenly in alarm, throw object, diffident, uneasy or wary in company
Slip	unintentional failing (e.g. error, loss of balance), loose cover (for person, furniture, etc.), artificial slope, travel unobserved
Table	item of furniture, information organized in columns
Tablet	slab of stone, drug in solid form
Tap	draw supplies or information, hit lightly, valve controlling flow (e.g. of water), sound (produced, e.g. by light knock on door)
Tend	incline towards, look after
Wake	funeral ritual, disturbance resulting from passage, e.g. of ship or aircraft, rise from sleep
Watch	period of wakefulness especially at night, personal chronometer, observe
Wax	sticky substance such as that produced by bees, apply such substance (e.g. to clean or protect surface), grow or increase
Vice	immoral or distasteful conduct or habit, device for securing object while working upon it
Yard	unit of measure, small enclosed area
Yarn	tale, thread

Appendix C: Words with More than One Pronunciation

The words listed below can take more than one spoken form depending upon how they are used. In general a change of vowel sound signifies a change of meaning; for example, the word "tear" can mean either a drop which falls from the eye (pronounced teer) or a break, rip or wound (pronounced tare). Changes in the placement of the stress generally indicate a change of usage from one part of language to another; for example, the word "record" is pronounced <u>re</u>-cord when it is used as a noun or an adjective but becomes re-<u>cord</u> when it is used as a verb.

The list below is not exhaustive, but is intended to give some idea of the range of such effects found in spoken English.

Absent	<u>ab</u>-sent	ab-<u>sent</u>
Abstract	<u>ab</u>-stract	ab-<u>stract</u>
Addict	<u>add</u>-ict	add-<u>ict</u>
Adept	<u>ad</u>-ept	ad-<u>ept</u>
Ally	<u>al</u>-ly	al-<u>ly</u>
Annex	<u>ann</u>-ex	ann-<u>ex</u>
Attribute	<u>att</u>-ri-bute	att-<u>ri</u>-bute
August	<u>aug</u>-ust	aug-<u>ust</u>
Bow	bo	bôw
Collect	<u>col</u>-lect	col-<u>lect</u>
Combat	<u>com</u>-bat	com-<u>bat</u>
Combine	<u>com</u>-bine	com-<u>bine</u>
Deliberate	de-lib-er-ate	de-lib-er-âte
Detail	<u>de</u>-tail	de-tail
Finance	<u>fi</u>-nance	fî-<u>nance</u>
Imprint	<u>im</u>-print	im-<u>print</u>
Incline	<u>in</u>-cline	in-<u>cline</u>

Indent	<u>in</u>-dent	in-<u>dent</u>
Insult	<u>in</u>-sult	in-<u>sult</u>
Intake	<u>in</u>-take	in-<u>take</u>
Intern	<u>in</u>-tern	in-<u>tern</u>
Interrupt	<u>in</u>-ter-rupt	in-ter-<u>rupt</u>
Intimate	inti-mate	inti-mâte
Lead	leed	lêd
Live	live	lîv
Mandate	<u>man</u>-date	man-<u>date</u>
Minute	<u>mîn</u>-it	mi-<u>newt</u>
Object	<u>ob</u>-ject	ob-<u>ject</u>
Perfect	<u>per</u>-fect	per-<u>fect</u>
Pervert	<u>per</u>-vert	per-<u>vert</u>
Read	reed	rêd
Rebel	<u>re</u>-bel	re-<u>bel</u>
Record	<u>re</u>-cord	re-<u>cord</u>
Row	ro	rôw
Second	<u>se</u>-cond	se-<u>cond</u>
Tear	tair	teer
Use	rhymes with fuse	rhymes with loose

Guide to Pronunciation

a= a as in ate	â= a as in at
e = e as in bead	ê = e as in bed
i = i as in lie	î = i as in lit
o = o as in go	ô = o as in brow

References

Allen J, Hunnicutt MS and Klatt DH (1987) *From Text to Speech: The MITalk System*, Cambridge University Press.

Arons B (1993) SpeechSkimmer: Interactively skimming recorded speech, *Proceedings of the Sixth ACM Symposium on User Interface Software and Technology*, Atlanta, USA, 3–5th November 1993, 187–196.

Ayres TJ, Jonides J, Reitman JS, Egan JC and Howard DA (1979) Differing suffix effects for the same physical suffix, *Journal of Experimental Psychology: Human Learning and Memory*, 5, 315–321.

Baber C, Arvanitis TN, Haniff DJ and Buckley R (1999) A wearable computer for paramedics: Studies in model-based, user-centred and industrial design, in *Proceedings of Interact 99*, MA Sasse and C Johnson (eds), IOS Press, Edinburgh, 126–132.

Baddeley AD (1966) Short term memory for word sequences as a function of acoustic, semantic and formal similarity, *Quarterly Journal of Experimental Psychology*, 18, 362–365.

Baddeley AD (1993) *Your Memory: A User's Guide*, Prion (Multimedia Books Ltd), London.

Bartlett FC (1932) *Remembering*, Cambridge University Press.

Begault DR and Erbe T (1994) Multichannel spatial auditory display for speech communications, *Journal of the Audio Engineering Society*, 42, 819–826.

Blattner M and Greenberg RM (1992) Communicating and learning through non-speech audio, in *Multimedia Interface Design in Education*, ADN Edwards and S Holland (eds), Springer-Verlag, Berlin, 133–144.

Blattner MM, Sumikawa DA and Greenberg RM (1989) Earcons and icons: their structure and common design principles, *Human–Computer Interaction*, 4(1), 11–44.

Blenkhorn P (1995) Producing a text-to-speech synthesizer for use by blind people, in *Extra-ordinary Human–Computer Interaction: Interfaces for Users with Disabilities*, ADN Edwards (ed.), Cambridge University Press, New York, 307–314.

Bly S (1982) *Sound and computer information presentation*, PhD Thesis, Report UCRL53282, Lawrence Livermore National Laboratory.

Bower GH, Clark MC, Lesgold AM and Winzenz D (1969) Hierarchical retrieval schemes in recall of categorized word lists, *Journal of Verbal Learning and Verbal Behaviour*, 8, 323–343.

Bransford JD and Johnson MK (1972) Contextual prerequisites for understanding: Some investigations of comprehension and recall, *Journal of Verbal Learning and Verbal Behaviour*, 11, 717–726.

Brewster SA (1994) *Providing a structured method for integrating non-speech audio into human–computer interfaces*, DPhil Thesis, Department of Computer Science, University of York, UK.

Brewster SA, Raty V-P and Kortekangas A (1995) *Representing complex hierarchies with earcons*, Technical report, ERCIM-05/95R037, ERCIM.

Brewster SA, Wright PC and Edwards ADN (1992) A detailed investigation into the effectiveness of earcons, auditory display, sonification, audification and auditory interfaces, in *Proceedings of the First International Conference on Auditory Display*, Santa Fe Institute, Santa Fe, G Kramer (ed.), Addison-Wesley, 471–498.

Broadbent DE, Cooper PJ and Broadbent MH (1978) A comparison of hierarchical matrix retrieval schemes in recall, *Journal of Experimental Psychology: Human Learning and Memory*, 4, 486–497.

Brown G (1983) Prosodic structure and the given/new distinction, in *Prosody: Models and Measurements*, A Cutler and DR Ladd (eds), Springer-Verlag, Berlin, 67–77.

Buxton W (1989) Introduction to this special issue on non-speech audio, *Human–Computer Interaction*, 4(1), 1–10.

Buxton W, Gaver W and Bly S (1991) *Tutorial Number 8: The Use of Non-speech Audio at the Interface*, ACM, New York.

Chafe WL (1970) *Meaning and the Structure of Language*, Chicago University Press, Chicago.

Conrad R (1960) Very brief delay of immediate recall, *Quarterly Journal of Experimental Psychology*, 12, 45–47.

Conrad R (1964) Acoustic confusion in immediate memory, *British Journal of Psychology*, 55, 75–84.

Cowan N, Litchi W and Grove T (1988) Memory for unattended speech during silent reading, in *Practical Aspects of Memory: Current Research and Issues*, Vol 2, *Clinical and Educational Implications*, MM Gruneberg, PE Morris and RN Sykes (eds), John Wiley & Sons, Chichester, 327–332.

Crowder RG (1967) Prefix effects in immediate memory, *Canadian Journal of Psychology*, 21, 450–461.

Crowder RG and Morton J (1969) Precategorical Acoustic Storage (PAS), *Perception and Psychophysics*, 5, 365–373.

Crystal D (1987) *The Cambridge Encyclopedia of Language*, Cambridge University Press.

Crystal D (1988) *Rediscover Grammar*, Longman, England.

Dahl O (1976) What is new information?, in *Reports on Text-Linguistics: Approaches to Word Order*, NE Enkvist and V Kohonen (eds), Text Linguistics Research Group, Abo.

Dallett KM (1965) Primary memory: The effects of redundancy upon digit reproduction, *Psychonomic Science*, 3, 237–238.

Darwin CJ, Turvey MT and Crowder RG (1972) An auditory analogue of the sperling partial report procedure: Evidence for brief auditory storage, *Cognitive Psychology*, 3, 255–267.

Duez D (1972) Silent and non-silent pauses in three speech styles, *Language and Speech*, 25, 11–28.

Dutoit T (1997) *An Introduction to Text-to-Speech Synthesis (Text, Speech and Language Technology*, V3), Kluwer Academic.

Edwards ADN (1991) *Speech Synthesis: Technology for Disabled People*, Paul Chapman, London.

Edwards ADN (1998a) Surfing and driving don't mix, *Interactions*, 5(3), 80 (http://www.acm.org/pubs/articles/journals/interactions/1998-5-3/p80-edwards/p80-edwards.pdf).

Edwards ADN (1998b) Access to mathematics for blind people: The maths project, *Maths & Stats*, 9(2), 14–15.

Edwards ADN (1998c) Mathematical access for technology and science for visually disabled people, http://www.cs.york.ac.uk/maths/

Edworthy J, Loxley S and Dennis I (1991) Improving auditory warning design: Relationships between warning sound parameters and perceived urgency, *Human Factors*, 33(2), 205–231.

Edworthy J, Loxley S, Geelhoed E and Dennis I (1989) The perceived urgency of auditory warnings, *Proceedings of the Institute of Acoustics*, 11(5), 73–80.

Engle RW (1974) The modality effect: Is precategorical audio storage responsible?, *Journal of Experimental Psychology*, 102, 824–829.

Gaver WW (1989) The SonicFinder: An interface that uses auditory icons, *Human–Computer Interaction*, 4(1), 67–94.

Gaver WW (1997) Auditory interfaces, in *Handbook of Human–Computer Interaction*, MG Helander, TK Landauer and P Prabhu (eds), Elsevier Science, Amsterdam, 1003–1042.

Gaver WW, Smith RB and O'Shea TM (1991) Effective sounds in complex systems: The arkola simulation, *Proceedings of CHI '91*, New Orleans, Addison-Wesley, 85–90.

Gill JM (1993) *A Vision of Technological Research for Visually Disabled People*, The Engineering Council, London WC2R 3ER.

Glucksberg S and Cowan GN (1970), Memory for non-attended auditory material, *Cognitive Psychology*, 1, 149–156.

Goldman-Eisler F (1972) Pauses, clauses, sentences, *Language and Speech*, 15, 103–113.

Grice HP (1975) Logic and conversation, in *Syntax and Semantics 3: Speech Acts*, P Cole and JL Morgan (eds), Seminar Press, New York.

Grosjean F and Deschamps A (1973) Analyse des variables Temporelles du Francais Spontane II Comparaison du Francais Oral dans la description avec l'Anglais (description) et avec le Francais (interview radiophonique), *Phonetica*, 28, 191–226.

Halliday MAK (1963) The tones of English, *Archives of Linguistics*, 15, 1–28.

Halliday MAK (1967a) Notes on transitivity and theme in English, part 2, *Journal of Linguistics*, 3, 199–244.

Halliday MAK (1967b) *Intonation and Grammar in British English*, Mouton, The Hague.

Halliday MAK (1970) *A Course in Spoken English: Intonation*, Oxford University Press, Oxford.

Jenkins JJ and Russell WA (1952) Associative clustering during recall, *Journal of Abnormal and Social Psychology*, 47, 818–821.

Johnson-Laird PN (1970) The interpretation of quantified sentences, in *Advances in Psycholinguistics*, GB Flores and WJM Levelt (eds), North-Holland, Amsterdam.

Keller E (ed.) (1994) *Fundamentals of Speech Synthesis and Speech Recognition: Basic Concepts, State of the Art and Future Challenges*, John Wiley & Sons.

Lodge N (1995) Television without the pictures: The work of audetel, *Technical review of the Asia Pacific Broadcasting Union*, 159 (http://www.itc.org.uk/uk_television_sector/accessibility/index.asp).

Loomis JM, Klatzky RL, Golledge RG, Cicinelli JC, Pellegrino JW and Fry PA (1993) Non-visual navigation by blind and sighted: Assessment of path integration ability, *Journal of Experimental Psychology: General*, 122, 73–91.

Luce PA (1982) Comprehension of fluent synthetic speech produced by rule, *Journal of the Acoustical Society of America*, 71, 1208–1221.

Luce PA, Feustel TC and Pisoni DB (1983) Capacity demands in short-term memory for synthetic and natural speech, *Human Factors*, 25(1), 17–32.

MacKay DG (1966) To end ambiguous sentences, *Perception and Psychophysics*, 1, 426–436.

Miller GA (1956) The magical number seven, plus or minus two: Some limits on our capacity for processing information, *Psychological Review*, 63, 81–97.

Moray N, Bates A and Barnett T (1965) Experiments on the four-eared man, *Journal of the Acoustical Society of America*, 38, 196–201.

Morton J and Long J (1976) Effect of word transition probability on phoneme identification, *Journal of Verbal Learning and Verbal Behaviour*, 15, 43–51.

Mukherjee R (1997) *The recognition of document categories based on non-speech audio*, MSc(IP) Project Report, Department of Computer Science, University of York, UK.

Murray DJ (1966) Vocalization at presentation and immediate recall with varying recall methods, *Quarterly Journal of Experimental Psychology*, 18, 9–18.

Mynatt ED, Back M, Want R and Frederick R (1997) Audio aura: Light-weight audio augmented reality, in *Proceedings of the Fourth International Conference on Audio Display* (ICAD '97), J Ballas and E Mynatt (eds), Xerox, Palo Alto, California, 105–107.

Nakatani LH and Schaffer J (1978) Hearing words without words: Prosodic cues for word perception, *Journal of the Acoustical Society of America*, 63, 234–244.

Nass C and Lee KM (2001) Does computer-synthesized speech manifest personality?, *Journal of Experimental Psychology: Applied*, 7(3), 171–181.

Nass C and Moon Y (2000) Machines and mindlessness: Social responses to computers, *Journal of Social Issues*, 56(1), 81–103.

Nusbaum HC and Pisoni DB (1985) Constraints on the perception of synthetic speech generated by rule, behaviour research methods, *Instruments & Computers*, 17(2), 235–242.

Patterson RD (1982) *Guidelines for Auditory Warning Systems on Civil Aircraft*, Report Paper 82017, Civil Aviation Authority.

Patterson RD (1989) Guidelines for the design of auditory warning sounds, *Proceeding of the Institute of Acoustics, Spring Conference*, 11(5), 17–24.

Penney CG (1975) Modality effects in short term verbal memory, *Psychological Bulletin*, 82, 68–84.

Penney CG (1979) Interactions of suffix effects with suffix delay and recall modality in serial recall, *Journal of Experimental Psychology*, 5, 507–521.

Penney CG (1989) Modality effects and the structure of short term verbal memory, *Memory & Cognition*, 17(4), 398–422.

Pitt IJ (1996) *The principled design of speech-based interfaces*, DPhil Thesis, Department of Computer Science, University of York, UK.

Pitt IJ and Edwards ADN (1996) Improving the usability of speech-based interfaces for blind users, *Proceedings of the ACM Conference on Assistive Technologies*, Vancouver, Canada, April 1996, 124–130.

Pitt IJ and Edwards ADN (1997) An improved auditory interface for the exploration of lists, *Proceedings of the 5th ACM International Multimedia Conference*, Seattle, USA, 8–14th November 1997, 51–61.

Pitt IJ (1998) From graphics to pure text, in *Abstraction in Computer Graphics*, T Strothotte (ed.), Springer-Verlag, Berlin, 177–195.

Posner MI and Rossman E (1965) Effect of size and location of informational transforms upon short-term retention, *Journal of Experimental Psychology*, 70, 496–505.

Postman L and Phillips LW (1965) Short-term temporal changes in free recall, *Quarterly Journal of Experimental Psychology*, 17, 132–138.

Poulton AS (1983) *Microcomputer Speech Synthesis and Recognition*, Sigma Technical Press, Wilmslow, Cheshire.

Prince EF (1981) Towards a taxonomy of given/new information, in *Radical Pragmatics*, P Cole (ed.), Academic Press, New York, 223–255.

Redelmeier DD and Tibshirani RJ (1997) Association between cellular-telephone calls and motor vehicle collisions, *New England Journal of Medicine*, 336(7), 453–458.

Reich S (1980) Significance of pauses for speech perception, *Journal of Psycholinguistic Research*, 9(4), 379–389.

Ribeiro N (2002) *Enhancing information awareness through speech induced anthropomorphism*, DPhil Thesis, Department of Computer Science, University of York, UK.

Robinson CP and Eberts RE (1987) Comparison of speech and pictorial displays in a cockpit environment, *Human Factors*, 29(1), 31–44.

Ryan J (1969) Temporal grouping, rehearsal and short-term memory, *Quarterly Journal of Experimental Psychology*, 21, 148–155.

Sawhney N and Schmandt C (1999) Nomadic radio: Scaleable and contextual notification for wearable audio messaging, in *The Chi is the Limit: Proceedings of Chi '99*, MG Williams, MW Altom, K Ehrlich and W Newman (eds), AC, 96–103.

Stevens R (1996) *Principles for the design of auditory interfaces to present complex information to blind computer users*, DPhil Thesis, Department of Computer Science, University of York, UK.

Stevens RD, Brewster SA, Wright PC and Edwards ADN (1994a) Providing an audio glance at algebra for blind readers, in *Auditory Display: Sonification, Audification and Auditory Interfaces: Proceedings of ICAD '94*, Santa Fe, G Kramer and S Smith (eds), Addison-Wesley, 21–30.

172

Stevens RD, Wright PC and Edwards ADN (1994b) Prosody improves a speech based interface, in *Ancillary Proceedings of HCI '94*, Loughborough, D England (ed.), British Computer Society.

Stevens RD, Wright PC, Edwards ADN and Brewster SA (1996a) An audio glance at syntactic structure based on spoken form, in *Interdisciplinary Aspects on Computers Helping People with Special Needs: Proceedings of the 5th International Conference, ICCHP '96*, Linz, J Klaus, E Auff, W Kremser and WL Zagler (eds), R Olenbourg, 627–635.

Stevens RD, Harling P and Edwards ADN (1996b) Reading and writing syntax trees for phrase structured grammars with a speech-based interface, in *New Technologies in the Education of the Visually Handicapped*, Paris, D Burger (ed.), John Libbey Eurotext, 271–276.

Stevens RD, Wright PC and Edwards ADN (1995) Strategy and prosody in listening to algebra, in *Adjunct Proceedings of HCI '95: People and Computers*, Huddersfield, G Allen, J Wilkinson and PC Wright (eds), British Computer Society, 160–166.

Streeter L (1978) Acoustic determinants of phrase boundary perception, *Journal of the Acoustical Society of America*, 64, 1582–1592.

ten Hoopen G (1996) Auditory attention, in *Handbook of Perception and Action*, O Neumann and A F Sanders (eds), Academic Press, London, 3, 79–112.

't Hart J and Cohen A (1973) Intonation by rule: A perceptual quest, *Journal of Phonetics*, 1, 309–327.

Tognazzini B (1992) *Tog on Interface*, Addison-Wesley.

Tulving E and Pearlstone Z (1966) Availability versus accessibility of information in memory for words, *Journal of Verbal Learning and Verbal Behaviour*, 5, 381–391.

Turing A (1950) Computing machinery and intelligence, *Mind*, 49, 433–460.

Vaissiere J (1983) Language-independent prosodic structures, in *Prosody: Models and Measurements*, A Cutler and DR Ladd (eds), Springer-Verlag, Berlin, 53–66.

Walker MA, Cahn JE and Whittaker SJ (1997) Improvising linguistic style: Social and affective bases for agent personality, *First International Conference on Autonomous Agents*, Marina Del Rey, ACM Press, 96–105.

Waterworth JA (1983) Effect of intonation form and pause durations of automatic telephone number announcements on subjective preference and memory performance, *Applied Ergonomics*, 14(1), 39–42.

Wicklegren WA (1964) Size of rehearsal group and short-term memory, *Journal of Experimental Psychology*, 68, 413–419.

Witten IH (1982) *Principles of Computer Speech*, Academic Press, London.

Yankelovitch N (1994) Talking versus taking: Speech access to remote computers, *Companion to the ACM CHI '94 Conference*, Boston, USA, April 24–28 1994.

Yankelovitch N, Levow G-A and Marx M (1995) Designing speech acts: Issues in speech user interfaces, *Proceedings of ACM CHI '95*, Denver, USA, May 7–11 1995, 369–376.

Zajicek M, Powell C, Reeves C and Griffiths J (1998) Web browsing for the visually impaired, in *Computers and Assistive Technology, ICCHP '98: Proceedings of the XV IFIP World Computer Congress*, Vienna & Budapest, ADN Edwards, A Arato and WL Zagler (eds), Austrian Computer Society, 161–169.

Zhang J (1996) A representational analysis of relational information displays, *International Journal of Human–Computer Studies*, 45, 59–74.

Index

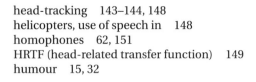

Published in association with the British Computer Society

Other titles in this series:

Practitioner Series

Springer

London
Berlin
Heidelberg
New York
Hong Kong
Milan
Paris
Tokyo